THIS IS MY BELOVED SON
THE TRANSFIGURATION OF CHRIST

Andreas Andreopoulos

Foreword by Metropolitan Kallistos of Diokleia

PARACLETE PRESS
BREWSTER, MASSACHUSETTS

This Is My Beloved Son: The Transfiguration of Christ

2016 Second Printing
2012 First Printing

ISBN 978-1-55725-656-0

            Library of Congress Cataloging-in-Publication Data
Andreopoulos, Andreas, 1966-
  This is my beloved Son : the transfiguration of Christ / Andreas
Andreopoulos ; foreword by Metropolitan Kallistos of Diokleia.
     p. cm.
  ISBN 978-1-55725-656-0 (trade pbk.)
  1. Jesus Christ—Transfiguration. I. Title.
  BT410.A53 2012
  232.9'56—dc23   2012003474

10 9 8 7 6 5 4 3 2

Published by Paraclete Press
Brewster, Massachusetts
www.paracletepress.com
Printed in the United States of America

TO FR. ANDREW LOUTH

...ὡς Ἀλέξανδρος ἔλεγε, τοῦ πατρός, ὡς δι᾽ ἐκεῖνον μὲν ζῶν,
διὰ Ἀριστοτέλην δὲ καλῶς ζῶν
—PLUTARCH, *Alexander*, 8:3

Alexander used to say that he owed to his father living,
but to [his teacher] Aristotle he owed living well.

CONTENTS

Wно is Christ? Who am I? For an answer, we may turn to one of the most mysterious events in the Gospels: the Transfiguration of Christ on the mountain in the presence of his three chosen disciples—Peter, James, and John. The dazzling light that shone from the face of Jesus reveals to us his true stature as the eternal Son of God. It reveals to us also the highest potentiality of our created nature, our ultimate vocation as human beings.

Andreas Andreopoulos has already written an earlier study on the Transfiguration, entitled *Metamorphosis*.[1] This has been widely acclaimed as an original and illuminating explanation of the theology and iconography of the Transfiguration, the fullest and most authoritative treatment of the subject available in the English language. In this present book he does not repeat what he has said so well in his earlier volume, but he approaches the Transfiguration from a different point of view, explaining its significance in the continuing experience of the church and in the personal journey of each Christian. He sees the Transfiguration as "a timeless story," as "an event that keeps on happening." He shows us how this moment in Christ's life has lived on through history, shedding its radiance upon all ages.

In the light of Christ's face that was so strangely and so strikingly altered upon the mountaintop, in his garments that became dazzling white, all human faces have acquired a new brightness, all common things have been transformed. For those who believe in Christ's Transfiguration, no one is despicable, nothing is trivial and mean. As Edwin Muir puts it in his poem "The Transfiguration":

The source of all our seeing rinsed and cleansed
Till earth and light and water entering there
Gave back to us the clear unfallen world.[2]

All this, and much more, Andreas Andreopoulos explains to us in the pages that follow. He writes in a way that is vivid yet profound and often unexpected. Reading his text, I have come to look at Christ's Transfiguration, and our own, with new eyes and a fresh understanding.

INTRODUCTION

I T IS HARD FOR ME TO WRITE ON MATTERS that neither my reason, nor my understanding, nor even my convictions have any hope of truly grasping. It is hard to take any part of the story of Jesus and explain it to others, as if I fully understand it myself, or to pretend to analyze it as if it were an abstract philosophical idea. But then, none of those abilities play any role in the presence of God. Instead, we can only try to respond in a way that recognizes his presence in the world, Scripture, life, and the sacraments of the church.

There are several books that examine the Transfiguration from a strictly biblical perspective or that discuss its reception and effect within early and later Christianity. There are also accounts of saints who experienced the continuous Transfiguration of Christ—the mystical experience of the outpouring of the light of God—as it was imparted to them. Here I did not want to restrict myself to the voice of knowledge or to the voice of experience. I tried to write partly with the approach of a theologian and teacher and partly with the approach of someone who tries to tell a story. But mostly, I approached the event from the perspective of a person who takes the narrative, the tradition, and the significance of the Transfiguration seriously at all levels.

I would not like to write a book as a diary of personal thoughts and experiences without recourse to a body of knowledge. This would not be useful to anyone. On the other hand, it is not enough to merely list what we know about the sources and the tradition of the Transfiguration, and exclude faith, understanding, and even intuition. Instead I tried to write as directly as I could and combine the two voices, drawing on what I know at both levels, neither hiding behind the persona of a teacher, nor resorting to an emotional or pietistic subjectivism. At both levels, however, my voice remains nothing more than a witness to a miracle that happened once, in a specific time and place, but still shines forth and reaches the world and the people of God.

It is hard to approach and consider the mystery of the Cross or the Resurrection, but perhaps these events are so big and so deeply embedded in history that our mind has a different way of dealing with them. The Crucifixion as the last public act of Jesus, and the Resurrection as the core of the Good News of the gospel, are events that decisively shaped Christianity. Momentous as they may be, we absorb and in some way accept them for what they are as we encounter the Christian faith and narrative for the first time. In this way they are not as surprising or unanticipated as some of the less prominent biblical narratives.

The story of the Transfiguration, on the other hand, communicates something more unexpected, something less embedded to our cultural acceptance of Christianity, and something that provokes a reading at a deeper, and yet more direct, level. It resonates in many ways with what we hear sometimes from elderly monks and charismatic laypeople, about a different kind of recognition of the presence of God, in a more palpable way—even when the light is so dazzling that you cannot know what it is that you are sensing. There is something immediate in this story, something that draws us inside of it, at the foot or on the top of Mount Thabor, where we can see Christ change into his real form, the form of light. Words cannot fully express the experience. I know, however, that the last thing I would need to do after such an event is to systematize it, classify it, or analyze it philosophically and theologically—at least if *theology* means what it usually means in our days. Yet, as with most experiences that lie beyond the level of the ordinary, we inevitably return to the words, to that part of thought that likes black to be black, and a table to be a table, and does not register easily that for which it does not have a word.

But then, we occasionally see a glow in the faces of some people that betrays an inner sense, a spiritual way to touch, see, and hear. This glow, humble and rare as it may be, does not appear only in the serene faces of the saints in iconography. Recently I heard someone speak about an elderly aunt of his, a simple woman who grew up in Asia Minor and came to Athens as a refugee in 1922. That woman used to take him to church with her when he was a child. Once, after communion, he saw her face shine in an unusual way, and naturally, with the curiosity and the directness of a young boy, he asked her what that was, why was her face glowing so strangely. He still remembers her response: closing in, and smiling almost conspiratorially, she told him, "Don't say anything, my child. It is a sin to talk about such things."

"Such things" cannot be described by words, and if nothing else that man's memory shows that sanctity is not an affair only of the past. Yet here I am, assuming the responsibility to talk and write about the Transfiguration in the background of "such things." This is not easy, I'll say this again. I find many such exhortations to silence in the lives of the saints. It is even right there in the biblical Transfiguration narrative itself, when Jesus instructs the three disciples who have seen what their eyes could not believe to keep silent about it until after his Crucifixion and his Resurrection, when the full mystery would be revealed to the entire world. This is one of several connections between Thabor and Calvary, the Transfiguration and the Cross. The message here is very strong: we cannot understand the glory of the Transfiguration or the Resurrection if we have not made the Cross part of our own life. Similarly, the command of Jesus to the disciples to keep this in silence until after they had known him as the crucified and resurrected God implies that the mystery of the Transfiguration cannot be approached as an inert object of study from the outside, without reverence, without fear, and without trembling. "Such things" are not spoken of lightly.

I know that in this attempt there may be times where all my education, my knowledge, and my wits can work against me. I am afraid that some of my thoughts or my phrases may escape and may try to have a life of their own, without a direct connection to things that resonate with my own experience. I am terrified that although I know that I have to walk on the crutches of my mind and my experiences, I'll drift instead toward the crutches of keeping fast on the way. But I cannot give up—not yet. I owe it to the few droplets of grace that I was made conscious of, or rather the few instances that made me aware of the continuous outpouring of grace.

And yet, this is not simply a personal difficulty that I acknowledge out of piety. The entire biblical message offers itself freely on this condition. I am reminded of St. Paul's self-imposed limitations, when he wrote, "Christ did not send me to baptize, but to preach the gospel, not with wisdom of words, lest the cross of Christ should be made of no effect" (1 Cor. 1:17). There is something misleading about an eloquent "wisdom of words" and "systematic" or scholarly theology, which as St. Paul testifies, stands at odds with the power of the Cross of Christ, and—I'll dare add—also at odds with his Transfiguration. Eloquent wisdom is a trap, a professional deformation into which theologians fall very often, perhaps more often than anyone else.

The reason for this is that Christianity is not a philosophical system, a set of rules and laws, or an intellectual edifice that attempts to explain the world to us. It is instead a way of life, an insight that flows out of living experience, which includes things we see, touch, and understand, and also things that we do not comprehend even if we see and touch them. Christianity is at its most essential in the mystical sound of the heartbeat of the church, the breath of its saints, and the presence of the Bridegroom Christ just on the other side of our senses

The continuous Transfiguration of Christ in the church is one of those things. And if this is difficult to visualize, we can start from the biblical message itself: if we put ourselves in the place of the three apostles who witnessed this miracle we would have no words to describe or explain it. The narratives are revealing and elusive at the same time. "His face shone like the sun" and his clothes "became shining, exceedingly white, like snow; such as no launderer on earth can whiten them" (Mt. 17:2; Mk. 9:3). There is a lot that serious analysis can tell us about these passages, but if we pause for a moment and try to visualize the raw experience, we come at a loss. And if we did manage to visualize it to some small extent, it would be even more difficult to describe it.

I think there is much I learned by approaching the Transfiguration, as well as the theological and biblical tradition in general, in the language of symbols and images. There is much in the Bible that can be understood in a lateral, iconological way. We can consider the image of Jesus in John 8:6, writing on the ground with his finger, when the adulterous woman is brought in front of him. This is the only instance where the Bible says that he ever wrote anything—and nobody was even interested in what he wrote. This is not an image of indifference, though, quite the opposite. Here we have a dispute about the Mosaic Law, and Jesus is invited by the scribes and Pharisees to offer his interpretation. What follows goes against the moralistic and legalistic understanding of sacred tradition, as it was held by the scribes and Pharisees. Does Jesus have the authority to do this? This is precisely what the image of him writing on the ground suggests. There is only one other instance in Scripture where God has written something with his finger: the two tablets of the law that was given to Moses were written "with the finger of God" (Exod. 31:18; Deut. 9:10). We can make the connection with Jesus in John 8 in an iconological way only. Here we have the image of Jesus the Teacher, whom the scribes and the Pharisees wanted to consult about a matter of the law. The Johannine narrative portrays him in this way precisely to show him as the origin of the Mosaic Law—and therefore what follows is given with the authority of God the Lawgiver. The image of Jesus stooping down and writing on the ground with his finger reveals much more than a historical or philological analysis of the passage would. Yet this is something we would understand only if we can start thinking in images. Perhaps in this way we respond to the mystery of God, at the same time we can try to preserve it.

This book may be described as my response to the mystery of the Transfiguration. A few years ago I wrote a book on the theology and iconography of the Transfiguration, for which I conducted a considerable amount of research in the writings of the Fathers as well as in hymnography and in visual sources. After its publication, however, I was left with a feeling of incompleteness, as if something inside me was trying to tell me that I needed to revisit the story of the Transfiguration with a wider perspective. Although the choice of the themes I develop here suggests an approach that is usual to textual and theological analysis and systematic theology, I think it serves the mystery of the Transfiguration better if it is recognized that its full reality hovers somewhere beyond the systematic approach. Like many other things in the church and the Christian tradition, what is important lies on just the other side of conscious perception—although not very far from it. The Transfiguration is a story of divine glory. There is no right or wrong way to approach it, because no approach can ever be enough. But at least by telling and retelling the story, exploring it with our minds and our hearts, we open ourselves to it and let the story take root inside us. Perhaps this is the best I could hope with my own theological explorations.

One final note: For biblical quotations I chose to use the *New King James Version* of the Bible, as perhaps the translation that flows more naturally in the English language. Nevertheless, I have modified the text of the NKJV in one way: the pronouns that refer to the person of Christ have been changed to the lowercase. This does not reflect a preference for a low Christology, but where biblical and liturgical texts are discussed I found it easier, and perhaps more correct theologically, to follow the grammar and the spirit of the original Greek, where no such differentiation between pronouns or grammatical types that refer to Christ and other persons exist.

1
IN YOUR LIGHT WE SHALL SEE LIGHT
Transfiguration Themes throughout the Bible

WHEN WE PREPARE TO TRAVEL TO A NEW PLACE, we try to collect as much information as we can about the journey. While in the past such endeavours were extremely difficult and people had to prepare meticulously for a trip to a distant land, it is much easier nowadays to find information about a destination, other travellers' detailed itineraries, reviews of services, and to make journey plans with a travel agent or through the Internet. Nevertheless, the basic plan remains the same.

We first try to find a map of the journey, something to give us an idea of the landscape, the rivers, lakes, seas, or mountains that we may have to cross, and especially if we travel by car, the highways and roads we need to take and the cities and towns we need to go through. It takes me much longer to learn a new city if I do not have a map reference for where everything is. In fact, I feel lost if I cannot actually position myself in a map—so that I know where I stand in reference to where I am going.

Christianity was understood from its beginning as a journey whose destination is the kingdom of heaven. The teachings, the traditions, the liturgy, and the doctrines are nothing more than travel directions in this journey, some of which come from people who have made part of the journey. The destination, however, is known only through God, and while it is necessary for us to have the will and desire to walk in the way of God, it is not our own strength that can carry us to the end, but the strength of the Holy Spirit. Nevertheless, in this metaphor of salvation as a journey, perhaps the closest thing we have to a map is the gospel.

The Transfiguration of Jesus Christ is an important landmark in this journey. It is a timeless story, a wonderful and miraculous episode from the life of Jesus Christ that reveals a lot about our own journey toward salvation. While this story starts with the incident witnessed by Peter, John, and James on the top of a mountain in Palestine sometime around the year 33 AD, the significance and the message of the Transfiguration extend much further than that.

The Transfiguration in Mark, Matthew, and Luke

While much of what makes Christianity what it is took place before and after the New Testament was written, most Christians would agree that what the Bible contains is a sufficient basis for our salvation. Although the word of God—or the "memoirs of the apostles," as an ancient writer refers to the Gospels—has a strong historical element, it is misleading to reduce the importance of the Gospels to the status of a historical source. They are more than that.

The Gospel narratives in the ancient church were written in order to be read aloud, heard, and prayed in the Eucharistic gatherings of the Christians. The Gospels are first of all liturgical texts, and they were compiled primarily for this reason. These texts took their shape in early Christian communities and eventually were chosen by the early church as authoritative writings because they helped the people of God prepare for their participation in the sacramental sharing of the body and the blood of Christ that followed, and the kingdom of heaven to which it led. For this reason, every reading from the Gospels reveals something about the kingdom of heaven.

When we read texts of Aeschylus, Shakespeare, or Ionesco, we are fully aware that their natural setting is the theater stage, and we try to imagine how they serve dramatic principles that are fulfilled in the theatre. Outside this framework there is much in the texts that does not make sense. Likewise, when we examine passages from the New Testament, it is good to keep in mind the reason for which they were written and the Eucharistic context in which they were received. The text reveals only part of the journey, but it is not the journey itself.

In that light, there is no better place to begin this journey than to turn our attention to the Gospel narratives that describe the Transfiguration of Jesus. The main narratives are Mark 9:2–10, Matthew 17:1–9, and Luke 9:28–36. In all of them it is also important to note how they are placed in the wider context of the Bible, and what other stories come before and after them.[3]

> Now after six days Jesus took Peter, James, and John, and led them up a high mountain apart by themselves; and he was transfigured before them. His clothes became shining, exceedingly white, like snow, such as no launderer on earth can whiten them. And Elijah appeared to them with Moses, and they were talking with Jesus. Then Peter answered and said to Jesus, "Rabbi, it is good for us to be here; and let us make three tabernacles: one for you, one for Moses, and one for Elijah"—because he did not know what to say, for they were greatly afraid. And a cloud came and overshadowed them; and a voice came out of the cloud, saying, "This is my beloved Son. Hear him!" Suddenly, when they had looked around, they saw no one anymore, but only Jesus with themselves. Now as they came down the mountain, he commanded them that they should tell no one the things they had seen, till the Son of Man had risen from the dead. So they kept this word to themselves, questioning what the rising from the dead meant. (Mk. 9:2–10)

Now after six days Jesus took Peter, James, and John his brother, led them up a high mountain by themselves; and he was transfigured before them. His face shone like the sun, and his clothes became as white as the light. And behold, Moses and Elijah appeared to them, talking with him. Then Peter answered and said to Jesus, "Lord, it is good for us to be here; if you wish, let us make here three tabernacles: one for you, one for Moses, and one for Elijah."

While he was still speaking, behold, a bright cloud overshadowed them; and suddenly a voice came out of the cloud, saying, "This is my beloved Son, in whom I am well pleased. Hear him!" And when the disciples heard it, they fell on their faces and were greatly afraid. But Jesus came and touched them and said, "Arise, and do not be afraid." When they had lifted up their eyes, they saw no one but Jesus only. Now as they came down from the mountain, Jesus commanded them, saying, "Tell the vision to no one until the Son of Man is risen from the dead." (MATT. 17:1–9)

<>

Now it came to pass, about eight days after these sayings, that he took Peter, John, and James and went up on the mountain to pray. As he prayed, the appearance of his face was altered, and his robe became white and glistening. And behold, two men talked with him, who were Moses and Elijah, who appeared in glory and spoke of his decease, which he was about to accomplish at Jerusalem. But Peter and those with him were heavy with sleep; and when they were fully awake, they saw is glory and the two men who stood with him. Then it happened, as they were parting from him, that Peter said to Jesus, "Master, it is good for us to be here; and let us make three tabernacles: one for you, one for Moses, and one for Elijah"—not knowing what he said. While he was saying this, a cloud came and overshadowed them; and they were fearful as they entered the cloud. And a voice came out of the cloud, saying, "This is my beloved Son. Hear him!" When the voice had ceased, Jesus was found alone. But they kept quiet, and told no one in those days any of the things they had seen. (Lk. 9:28–36)

The story in these narratives is very direct and powerful. Mark and Matthew get right to the point. The first sentence connects the main Transfiguration story with the biblical text that precedes it: here we hear that Jesus took Peter, John, and James separately from the other disciples and led them to a mountain whose name is not given. Then both evangelists say simply that Jesus "was transfigured in front of them." They add that his clothes became resplendent white. Matthew also writes that his face shone like the sun. Other than that, there is no attempt to explain what exactly the word *transfigured* means, as if the meaning and the special way in which this Transfiguration happened is already known to the people who hear the story. Luke's Gospel, on the other hand, takes a slightly softer tone: it does not simply announce the Transfiguration, but it describes the change of the face of Jesus and his clothes.

If we place ourselves in the gathering of the faithful, where these texts would have been read aloud and prayed in the Eucharistic gathering, we immediately realize that they guide us into something unusual, something that has little to do with what Jesus says, and more with what he does or what happens to him. There is much that is not given in words here. There is a lot that is not explained.

The whole story has something elusive about it, making it sound like a shared secret. The separate ascent to the mountain, the white cloud, the mysterious light, the voice from heaven, and any of the other parts of the story are not described in detail. The texts have an incomplete feel to them: the events are related almost in hurry, as if the evangelists have given up hope to do justice to the description of the event with their words.

In the context of the Eucharistic gathering, the Transfiguration narrative reveals to a community of believers an additional aspect of the kingdom of God. Those who hear these Gospel texts are hearing them already present together as the community of God in Christ. They are there for the sacraments of the church, for the grace that comes from God through the *ecclesia*, and hearing these readings they understand that an important event took place long ago. Taken by themselves (without St. Paul—as we will soon see), the Transfiguration as an event can be confusing. It is important to remember, then, that this teaching is intended to prepare the way for the partaking of the sacramental body and blood of Christ. When the Gospel of the Transfiguration is read in the Eucharistic gathering, the whole day is a feast and a celebration of the Transfiguration, including especially composed services of Vespers and Matins, with many hymns dedicated to it. After the reading of the Gospel and the sermon, very few other things will remind us of the Transfiguration. The focus shifts to the experience of the sacramental resurrected body of Christ.

Let us consider this passage from later in the canon of the New Testament, as well. The Transfiguration is also mentioned in the second epistle of Peter:

> For we did not follow cunningly devised fables when we made known to you the power and coming of our Lord Jesus Christ, but were eyewitnesses of his majesty. For he received from God the Father honor and glory when such a voice came to him from the Excellent Glory: "This is my beloved

Son, in whom I am well pleased." And we heard this voice which came from heaven when we were with him on the holy mountain. And so we have the prophetic word confirmed, which you do well to heed as a light that shines in a dark place, until the day dawns and the morning star rises in your hearts. (2 PET. 1:16–19)

The style of the passage from 2 Peter is more straightforward than the story as told in the Gospels, because it was composed as a letter rather than as a somewhat cryptic liturgical reading. While the author mentions the Transfiguration as an example of the glory of God experienced directly by the apostles, his narrative culminates in the phrase we "were eyewitnesses of his majesty" (2 Pet. 1:16), which corresponds very closely with the phrase "we beheld his glory" that we find in John 1:14.[4] The text does not go into historical or narrative details, but it assumes that what it alludes to is already widely known to its readers. This suggests that although the Gospels as we know them were most likely written after this letter, Christian communities were already familiar with the Transfiguration, and that it was known as a revelation of the glory and the majesty of Christ. This letter is not trying to convince us that the Transfiguration took place; on the contrary, the author refers to the Transfiguration, which Peter experienced firsthand, as an undisputed fact, which he then proceeds to use as a source of hope and inspiration for his readers.

What about John?

Given all of this discussion in the Scriptures about the Transfiguration, why is it that John the Evangelist, the only person among the three eyewitnesses whose name is connected with a Gospel, did not write a Transfiguration narrative? The Gospel according to John—the last of the Gospels to be written—only briefly mentions that "we beheld his glory" (Jn. 1:14), which is usually understood as an allusion to the

Transfiguration, because the word *glory* (δόξα)[5] is immediately recognizable as an almost tangible manifestation of the divinity of Christ (such as we see in the Transfiguration), and not simply as an abstract and generic reference to the power and majesty of God. This becomes more obvious in Greek iconography, where the luminous aureole drawn around the body of Christ in icons of special metaphysical and unusual events that accentuate his divinity (such as the Transfiguration, the Resurrection, and the Ascension) is also known as "glory" (δόξα). Not only in a biblical context, but in a wider cultural context, the glory of God in the Greek tradition is understood as something visible.

But why does John's Gospel not specifically mention the Transfiguration? One theory has it that this Gospel was not actually written by John, the brother of James and son of Zebedee. If this is true, the author of the fourth Gospel was not present at the Transfiguration. But even if this were so, it is unlikely that he would not have heard of it. In addition, the entire fourth Gospel is concerned with many of the themes we find in the Transfiguration story: this Gospel, after all, is the Gospel of glory and divinity! The Passion in John, for instance, is not a moment of defeat or suffering, but a manifestation of Christ as the *King of Glory*, the title that we see written above the head of Christ in the Orthodox icon of the Crucifixion. The words *glory, glorification,* and *glorify* in John's Gospel have a specific meaning that is so evident it is clearly understood by all who hear the relevant Gospel reading. When in John's Gospel we read that Jesus says, "Father, the hour has come. Glorify your Son, that your Son also may glorify you" (Jn. 17:1) or, "This he spoke, signifying by what death he would glorify God" (Jn. 21:19), there is very little doubt in our mind that the Crucifixion is seen as an act of glory.

We come across the theme of divine light in the very first paragraph of John's Gospel, and in others as well. This interest in the theology of light is evident, more directly than anywhere else, in Christ's own words in John

8:12: "I am the light of the world. He who follows me shall not walk in the darkness, but have the light of life." This emphasis on light became the basis for a good part of the early discussion of the relationship between the Father and the Son and is something we find developed in a different way in John's Gospel than in Matthew, Mark, and Luke.

The particular themes that characterize John—light, glory—suggest that the entire book echoes the event of the Transfiguration. In other words, John's Gospel does not retell the Transfiguration story because the theme of the glory of God and the divine light permeate everything in it. The Transfiguration in the other three Gospels demonstrates the divinity of Christ and explains something of its nature to us in a dramatic, visual way. But John's Gospel begins differently, taking the divinity of Christ as something that needs no demonstration or proof, and is stated clearly right from the beginning.

If we were compelled to find an appropriate place to interject the narrative of the Transfiguration into John's Gospel, we could think of two possibilities. First, we may be inclined to place it at the end of chapter 6, right after Peter's confession of faith. This would be consistent with the very similar confession of faith that Peter gives just before the Transfiguration story in Mark, Matthew, and Luke and would make the Transfiguration narrative correspond with the reference to the Jewish Feast of the Tabernacles in John 7, where Jesus taught in the temple at the middle of the feast. Interestingly, several scholars have noticed a certain connection between the Feast of the Tabernacles and the Transfiguration of Jesus.[6] Yet this addition would not offer anything to the message of John's Gospel there. While in the following three chapters Jesus speaks publicly about the law and the prophets—and in an indirect sense he "dialogues" with Moses and Elijah, who encapsulate the Hebrew tradition—there is no attempt to demonstrate his divinity to the bystanders, as he teaches with the authority of the Father (Jn. 10:38), and yet they do not accept him.

We may also be tempted to place the Transfiguration story in the first opening paragraphs of John's Gospel. In John 1:14, the Evangelist writes about how "the Word became flesh and dwelt among us, and we beheld his glory, the glory as of the only begotten of the Father, full of grace and truth." This phrase connects glory with divinity, and it says something similar to the demonstration of the divinity of Christ precisely as we see it in the Transfiguration. This also could explain why there is no specific mention of the Transfiguration in John's Gospel later on. Since this Gospel starts with the writer's confession of faith and the testimony to the divinity and the glory of Christ, everything that follows is based on this testimony. In a certain sense, all of John is offered within the light of the Transfiguration.

Nevertheless, it is not usually prudent to compare John's Gospel with the other three Gospels. As a liturgical text it is read in the same way as the other three Gospels, and yet its content is more overtly Eucharistic. What I mean is, although there is no specific mention of the Last Supper and the historical institution of the Eucharistic meal here, it is possible to read the entire Gospel as a description and commentary of the Eucharistic rite—right from the beginning, where instead of a genealogy the Gospel begins with a hymn to Christ the Logos. In other words, the whole Gospel takes place in the transfigured space that is beyond the ascent to Mount Thabor.

The Transfiguration in St. Paul

There are two more, albeit indirect, references to the Transfiguration given in the New Testament. Rather, these are two instances where the theme of the Transfiguration exists in the background without direct reference to the Transfiguration of Jesus on Mount Thabor. In both we find the verb *transfigure* (μεταμορφώ) used in a way that implies this connection.

Both are found in the epistles of St. Paul, in Romans 12:2 and 2 Corinthians 3:18. In order to understand these references, we have to read each of them in their broader contexts:

> I beseech you therefore, brethren, by the mercies of God, that you present your bodies a living sacrifice, holy, acceptable to God, which is your reasonable service. And do not be conformed to this world, but be transfigured by the renewing of your mind, that you may prove what is that good and acceptable and perfect will of God.
>
> For I say, through the grace given to me, to everyone who is among you, not to think of himself more highly than he ought to think, but to think soberly, as God has dealt to each one a measure of faith. For as we have many members in one body, but all the members do not have the same function, so we, being many, are one body in Christ, and individually members of one another. Having then gifts differing according to the grace that is given to us, let us use them: if prophecy, let us prophesy in proportion to our faith; or ministry, let us use it in our ministering; he who teaches, in teaching; he who exhorts, in exhortation; he who gives, with liberality; he who leads, with diligence; he who shows mercy, with cheerfulness. (ROM. 12:1–8)

◁▷

> And we have such trust through Christ toward God. Not that we are sufficient of ourselves to think of anything as being from ourselves, but our sufficiency is from God, who also made us sufficient as ministers of the new covenant, not of the letter but of the Spirit; for the letter kills, but the Spirit gives life.

But if the ministry of death, written and engraved on stones, was glorious, so that the children of Israel could not look steadily at the face of Moses because of the glory of his countenance, which glory was passing away, how will the ministry of the Spirit not be more glorious? For if the ministry of condemnation had glory, the ministry of righteousness exceeds much more in glory. For even what was made glorious had no glory in this respect, because of the glory that excels. For if what is passing away was glorious, what remains is much more glorious.

Therefore, since we have such hope, we use great boldness of speech—unlike Moses, who put a veil over his face so that the children of Israel could not look steadily at the end of what was passing away. But their minds were blinded. For until this day the same veil remains unlifted in the reading of the Old Testament, because the veil is taken away in Christ. But even to this day, when Moses is read, a veil lies on their heart. Nevertheless when one turns to the Lord, the veil is taken away. Now the Lord is the Spirit; and where the Spirit of the Lord is, there is liberty. But we all, with unveiled face, beholding as in a mirror the glory of the Lord, are being transfigured into the same image from glory to glory, just as by the Spirit of the Lord. (2 COR. 3:4–18)

◇

In both of these passages we find something different about the use of the word *transfigured*.[7] For the first time in the New Testament, both the word and the concept are not associated with Jesus. Instead, they point to the members of the church, the ones who receive the word of instruction. Yet the context that connects the usage of these words to the Transfiguration of Jesus Christ is unmistaken.

In the passage from the Epistle to the Romans, St. Paul develops the theme of the transfiguration of the individual members of the church into the body of Christ. It is the same theme we find in one of his most famous passages, in 1 Corinthians 12, where he reflects on the different roles of the members of the body, and the different gifts of the Holy Spirit. What makes the unity of this ecclesial body possible, Paul insists, is baptism and the operation of the Holy Spirit (1 Cor. 12:13). In the Romans passage he describes the effect of baptism: it makes Christians "not conform to the world," but "be transfigured" from individuals to members of the body of Christ.

St. Paul shows us what the meaning of the Transfiguration is beyond its historical context. Although the historical Transfiguration of Jesus on Mount Thabor is present in the background of his words, Paul chooses to talk about another kind of Transfiguration of the body of Jesus Christ, where the body of Christ is understood in a different way. Here he is talking about the church as the body of Christ, and the Transfiguration of the church into his body. Paul is emphatic: the Transfiguration is not an event that belongs to the distant past, irrelevant to the life of the faithful. Instead, he helps us see the Transfiguration event from a different perspective: what happens to Christ also happens to us, to the church. This passage builds on the connection between Christ and the church and it guides us to understand and apply the biblical message beyond the confines of historical time.

In the passage from St. Paul's second letter to the Corinthians we see a stronger connection with the Transfiguration story. Here he refers to Moses as a "type" or precursor of Jesus and the revelation he was given as a preparation for the full revelation of God in Christ. Paul talks about the transfiguration of the face of Moses in Exodus 34:29–35, after Moses' encounter with God on Sinai, a story that is directly related to the Transfiguration of Christ. Paul mentions the "glory" of the face of Moses, which was a reflection of the glory or divine promise of the

Old Testament. He reminds us that the face of Moses had to be covered. According to the Exodus narrative, the Israelites could not bear to
look at his resplendent face directly, and for this reason it was covered
by a veil. In the story of the Transfiguration, the glory of the face of
Christ is the fulfillment of the radiance of the face of Moses. The veil
is removed and the glory of God is revealed completely and directly. If
in the Transfiguration there is a limitation to what can be seen, it is not
imposed to us by God, but by our limited nature.

St. Paul touches here on some of the main themes that have been
developed through the last two thousand years regarding the spiritual
importance of the Transfiguration for the lives of Christians. One of
them has to do with the nature of the change that occurred on the top
of that "high mountain." Jesus did not change who he was; he was God
before, during, and after his Transfiguration, as he was during his entire
ministry, fully divine and fully human. What changed was the percep-
tive capability of the apostles. Each of them was given the grace to see
and hear differently, and because of that they were able to see Jesus in
a different way. To the extent that Transfiguration means a change of
something into something that it was not before the change, the actual
transfiguration happened in Peter, John, and James, and not in Jesus.

This is something that St. Paul understands clearly. He considers
the Transfiguration of Jesus a prefiguration, a "mirror" of the human
condition, and he places us against the mirror (another of his recurring
themes, reminding us of how we see God "in a mirror, dimly" in 1
Corinthians 13) as a way to begin our own transfiguration into the
image and the glory of God. The phrase "we are being transfigured
into the same image from glory to glory" with which he concludes this
passage is one that encapsulates in a few words the mystery and the
nature of our salvation and our way into the light of God.

The passages from the epistles of St. Paul, as well as the passage from 2
Peter, reflect a practical and direct exhortation toward the Christian life.

This is where the historical event meets the life of every Christian. These passages help us relate the mystery of the Transfiguration of Christ directly to our lives.

There is a practical explanation for why we discover the spiritual meaning in the theology of the Transfiguration in this way—as St. Paul and St. Peter reflect on the event in the Gospels. These letters were written in order to address certain problems that the Christian communities were facing. For this reason they are less concerned with the story of Jesus and the revelation of the kingdom of God, and more with our spiritual struggle in this world. The church, recognizing this distinction, has always placed the liturgical reading of the epistles before the reading of the Gospel. St. Paul and St. Peter help to explain the broader, everyday, spiritual meaning of the event depicted for history in the Gospel texts. Liturgically, then, we are prepared to offer ourselves to be transfigured into the body of Christ at the same time we prepare to receive his own transfigured and resurrected body. The kingdom of God may lie just ahead, and it may be offered to us as freely and unconditionally as the light of God and the grace of the Holy Spirit was given to Peter, John, and James, but our entire life on earth can be spent trying to hold on to a morsel of this free gift of love.

The Transfiguration Offers a Key to Understanding the Whole Bible

Examining the Transfiguration story in the Gospels of Mark, Matthew, Luke, and the letters of Paul, as well as the resonance between the Transfiguration story and John's Gospel, we gain a certain appreciation for the revelation of Jesus Christ in Scripture. St. Maximos the Confessor, one of the most important theologians of the medieval church, wrote that the garments of Christ, which became resplendent at his Transfiguration, were symbolic of the pages of the Gospel as they will become clear to us at the end of time. For St. Maximos this

deep connection between the Gospel and Christ became apparent in
the divine light of the Transfiguration.

Christians of all denominations look to the Bible as an indispensable
base of their faith. Yet this is a living faith. The Bible is not received as a
stagnant document, but as one of the most important guides that reveal
to us Jesus Christ as the living God and witness his continuous presence in the church. The Transfiguration story explores in a few lines the
limits of his presence and revelation through Scripture, and the way this
revelation affects all Christians whose life is transfigured in prayer. It is
a story with many levels, and it can show us how deep the revelation of
Christ is.

The story of the Transfiguration, as most of the miracles, teachings,
and other events from the life of Christ, is revealed at different levels.
We start with Christ as he is revealed to us through the New Testament,
in the testimony of the Gospels. But after we enter the story at this point,
we may also read the Old Testament as a prophetic book that paves the
way for the revelation of Christ. The early church saw a prefiguration
of the Transfiguration of Christ in the shining face of Moses, when he
came down from Mount Sinai—and thus was able to discern a deeper
meaning in this event from Exodus. Moses and Elijah, who appeared
with Jesus in the mountain of the Transfiguration, represent the partial
revelation of God that was given to them and to the people of the Old
Testament, which could only be given fully in Christ. Therefore, when
we consider the plight of the Israelites in the desert, or the prophets who
spurned kings and rulers for their lack of faith and talked to them about
God, we can reflect on the fullness of the presence of God, which we
knew after he was born as a human being.

Of course the biblical stories are never simply pieces of information.
Even to read them with an open mind and heart is not enough. We
can remember here a short story from the eighth chapter of the book
of Acts, which mentions an Ethiopian dignitary who was reading

the prophecy of Isaiah while he was in his chariot. Philip the deacon heard him and asked, "Do you understand what you are reading?" The Ethiopian's response was, "How can I, unless someone guides me?" He was right, and the acknowledgment of his weakness was the first step in his journey from the words to the Word. Following this, Philip told the Ethiopian dignitary things that the book could not tell him, and led him to a faith that he could not reach on his own. He explained to him how the fulfilment of the prophecy of Isaiah was Jesus Christ, and how Christ was the deeper meaning of the book.

We are in the same position as the Ethiopian dignitary. For this reason the theology and the tradition of the church and the inspiration of the Holy Spirit are indispensible tools in our attempt to penetrate Scripture. It is not reason, knowledge, or information that can lead us to the end, only the operation of the Holy Spirit; and in the tradition of the church, its ascetics and Fathers, we do not recognize a chain of wise people who put their heads together; we only recognize the manifestation of the Holy Spirit that shone despite the limitations of the men in whom it was manifested.

We thought of Scripture in general as the map of the journey toward salvation. Well, the story of the Transfiguration is more than one of the areas on the surface of that map. It is also part of the map legend, the apparatus we need to read the map correctly. As such, in the Transfiguration we can see several ways to approach Christ, but we can also discern the inner connection of these approaches. All of those ways reveal something true about Christ, but we are better prepared for the journey toward salvation when we consider all of them. When we prepare for a journey, we take note of the map, but we also consult a travel guide. And if we get conflicting information from our sources, we start wondering whether we read the map correctly or whether we consulted the travel guide for London, Ontario, instead of the guide for London, England. It is the same with the several ways of approaching Christ. There should not be a difference in the way our sources and the pillars of our faith guide us, and for this reason, by considering them next to each other, we learn to read them correctly. Jesus Christ, who reveals himself in the Transfiguration, is the historical Jesus who was born in Bethlehem of Judea, but he is also the Word of God. He is the one who will come at the end of time in clouds of glory, and also the Christ whose sacramental body is the church. Considering all of these aspects at the same time reveals to us something about how the Bible should be read.

Looking toward the Transfigured Christ

The Gospels and the Transfiguration narratives were not written as if they were chronicles or historical documents, even though they have value as witnesses to real events. Today we do not have the benefit of meeting people who witnessed the Transfiguration firsthand, or people who met the eyewitnesses, but we accept the testimony of the Bible in trust and faith. Simply put, by believing the Gospel of Jesus Christ and the Transfiguration story, we believe that he revealed his divinity to his disciples in a miraculous event. We believe that this event was real and not symbolic, abstract, allegorical, or metaphorical. However, this is about as far as our historical aspiration can take us. The Gospels omit details that may be important for the historian. But they also describe events in such a way that allows us to understand them beyond the plain narrative.

The Transfiguration story is told in a slightly different way in Mark, Matthew, and Luke, which emphasize different aspects of the same event. The three narratives start with a mention of a certain time that passed after Peter's confession of faith—six days in Mark and Matthew, and eight in Luke. The early church tradition observed that while Mark and Matthew referred to the days that intervened between the two events, not counting the first and the last day, Luke, whose cultural background was different, calculated this time adding the first and the last day, as it was usual to him. Both accounts, according to this interpretation, correspond to what we would today think of "after a week." This may indeed be the case. Yet there is something more important here. All three evangelists felt that it was important to preface the Transfiguration story with a number that refers to the days of Creation, or to the Eighth Day—the day that Christian tradition identifies with the end of time, and with liturgical time. This detail, which does not need historical corroboration because its meaning is not historical, directs our attention to treat what we will read or hear about the Transfiguration as an event whose significance escapes the confines of time and space.

While we accept that the Word of God entered human history with his Incarnation and everything he did for us, we can keep in mind that the Bible itself gives us the incentive to read the Jesus story at a deeper level. A theology of the Transfiguration allows us to do just that.

We will return again to each of these themes in the chapters to come:

REVELATION OF THE LOGOS

In the Transfiguration story Christ lifted the curtain of his humanity and revealed his divinity. The Word of God, who accepted to unite with human nature, showed to Peter, John, and James that he was not only the son of Mary, born in Bethlehem and raised in Nazareth, but also that he was the pre-eternal God. This is the tone that permeates the beginning of John's Gospel and the reference to "the glory as of the only begotten of the Father" in John 1:14.

This revelation of the divinity of Christ reminds us that the Gospel is not the story of a man, but the story of God who became human while never ceasing to be God. Christ did not do anything out of necessity or need, but by choice. This realization becomes more important when we consider the significance of the Passion of Christ. Christ prepared his disciples to understand it by his Transfiguration. In this way, even at the moment of suffering and death, the Christ of the Crucifixion was not a powerless and defeated human, but the same glorious Christ that Peter, John, and James had already seen at the Transfiguration.

In other parts of the Gospel we see, likewise, images of Christ that emphasize his human nature and remind us that he embraced completely the human condition. Jesus asks for water; he weeps at the news of Lazarus' death; he complains that there is no place for him to rest his head; he sweats blood the night before his Crucifixion. These examples show that he was as fully human as any of us. Yet the Transfiguration reminds us that Christ, the Logos of God before the ages, united with human nature by his own choice. The glorious Word of God was humbled, but not humiliated by becoming human.

THE SECOND COMING

From a Christian perspective, all of Hebrew Scripture until the time of Jesus had one purpose only: to communicate the preparation for Christ's First Coming. Likewise, then, the single purpose of the New Testament and the tradition of the Christian church in this age is to prepare for the Second Coming of Christ.

Although the Second Coming is described in the book of Revelation and in Matthew 25, it is the Transfiguration that provides a more direct visual model for the glorious Christ of the Second Coming. The light that shone from his face bridged the gap between the present age and the end of time.

We know Christ as Savior because he unites the eternal nature of God with our mortal nature. This union allows us to participate in the eternity and in the inexhaustible source of life in God, and this is how we ultimately understand salvation. The Transfiguration of Christ is a historical event that points toward the time outside time, the end of days, the Second Coming, and the kingdom of heaven. Following the luminous Christ, we hope to fulfill our future in the transfiguring light of God.

The Transfiguration of Christ is also a marker that reminds us that the map of all of Scripture corresponds to the journey toward salvation. When we read about the teachings, the miracles, or the other events of the life of Christ in the New Testament, and also when we read about the prophecies, the kings, and the leaders of Israel in the Old Testament, it helps us to understand all those things better if we think of the image of the Transfigured Christ as a visual note in the margins of every page, as a reminder of the end of the journey.

THE TRANSFIGURED CHURCH

The divine drama of Christ did not end with his Ascension, when he was raised to the heavens and exited historical time. After the Ascension, Christ is still present in the church, but in a different way. The next stage of the divine drama was Pentecost, when the Holy Spirit started forming the sacramental body of Christ (as it was understood by St. Paul), from the body of the faithful. In other words, the Transfiguration of Christ is the model for the transfiguration of the individual members into his body. This means that as members of the body of Christ, we live his life. We are crucified with Christ when we celebrate and internalize his Crucifixion. We are resurrected with him when we celebrate his Resurrection. And we are transfigured with him when we celebrate his Transfiguration. We become Christ when we receive his sacramental resurrected body and blood, and this is our personal transfiguration into him. We fulfill the work of the church when we become Christ, when we are transfigured into his mystical body. The transfiguration of the self into the sacramental body of Christ was a continuous experience and calling for the early Christians, when St. Paul was calling them to be transfigured into Christ, even before the New Testament was being formed. It still is today.

2
THIS IS MY BELOVED SON, IN WHOM I AM PLEASED
Transfiguration as the Essence of the Christian Life

T HERE IS A FOLKTALE IN THE TRADITION OF CRETE that narrates how musicians learn to play. After an older musician shows a younger musician how to count notes, how to keep the rhythm, and how to use his fingers, the young one still does not know how to improvise, how to use his instrument in order to explore his feelings, how to inspire and how to touch the others. There is something in music that cannot be learned in the same way we learn a piece of information. And yet, the young musician wants to learn, to really learn, how to play. What does the legend say?

The young musician takes his *lyra* (this is the most expressive of all Cretan instruments) and finds a crossroads outside the village in the night. Using a piece of chalk, he writes a circle on the ground and stays inside. At midnight all sorts of beautiful spirits come, nymphs and fairies and anything else that the world of folktales knows. These spirits bring their instruments with them and play for the young musician the whole night. They try to get him to step out of the magic circle that protects him. The musicians who do so are taken by the spirits and never heard from again. The spirits play joyfully, they play sadly, they stir all sorts of emotions with their magical music, trying to enchant the young musician outside his safety. And when dawn comes, they have no option but to give up. They vanish into the air from which they came.

What has changed in the musician? He heard music that no human ear hears. And for the rest of his life he tries to play like the nymphs, to play the music he heard from them. This, the legend says, is what makes him a musician.

Our Christian lives are like this. We start out with baptism, a deeply significant ritual that symbolizes nothing less than our death and regeneration, but as the music of the nymphs is to the young musician, we keep coming back to that ritual as adults, trying to make more sense of it. We try to make it a little more real every time.

In the Orthodox Church we still practice baptism of babies by immersing them completely in water three times. This is sometimes difficult to watch, and there is no parent who has not felt uneasy at the baptism of their child. But the content of this rite, which is visually intense in its primitive form, is far more intense than the rite itself. Dramatic as the rite can be, it is nothing less than a riddle and a mystery that we are given as infants. Then we try to live up to it as much as we can for the rest of our lives.

This is a mystery of our change in Christ, of dying and being reborn in him. The Christian life is a continuous struggle to enter the mystery of our death and regeneration in Christ, of our transfiguration into members of Christ. We died and were reborn in the baptistery, in the hope of fulfilling St. Paul's "it is no longer I who live, but Christ lives in me" (Gal. 2:20). From that moment on, every time we break the limits of our egoism we die a little bit further. Every time we push away pride and conceit from our life, we find it painful. But this is when we clear the space and invite the Holy Spirit inside us. We start with our fallen nature, misguided, confused, sinful, and we hope that with the grace and the help of God we will offer it completely to Christ, changed and transformed according to his image.

The actualization of our baptism is a process of transformation in Christ, a transfiguration in him that has a lot in common with his own

Baptism and Transfiguration. For this reason, as we try to understand the significance of the Transfiguration of Jesus Christ for us, we should extend our view and explore the significance of his Baptism.

The Baptism of Christ in the Gospels

All four Gospels tell of it:

> John was clothed with camel's hair and with a leather belt around his waist, and he ate locusts and wild honey. And he preached, saying, "There comes one after me who is mightier than I, whose sandal strap I am not worthy to stoop down and loose. I indeed baptized you with water, but he will baptize you with the Holy Spirit."
>
> It came to pass in those days that Jesus came from Nazareth of Galilee, and was baptized by John in the Jordan. And immediately, coming up from the water, he saw the heavens parting and the Spirit descending upon him like a dove. Then a voice came from heaven, "You are my beloved Son, in whom I am well pleased." (Mk. 1:6–12)

◇

> I indeed baptize you with water unto repentance, but he who is coming after me is mightier than I, whose sandals I am not worthy to carry. He will baptize you with the Holy Spirit and fire. His winnowing fan is in his hand, and he will thoroughly clean out his threshing floor, and gather his wheat into the barn; but he will burn up the chaff with unquenchable fire."
>
> Then Jesus came from Galilee to John at the Jordan to be baptized by him. And John tried to prevent him, saying, "I need to be baptized by you, and are you coming to me?"

But Jesus answered and said to him, "Permit it to be so now, for thus it is fitting for us to fulfill all righteousness." Then he allowed him. When he had been baptized, Jesus came up immediately from the water; and behold, the heavens were opened to him, and he saw the Spirit of God descending like a dove and alighting upon him. And suddenly a voice came from heaven, saying, "This is my beloved Son, in whom I am well pleased." (Matt. 3:11–17)

◇

When all the people were baptized, it came to pass that Jesus also was baptized; and while he prayed, the heaven was opened. And the Holy Spirit descended in bodily form like a dove upon him, and a voice came from heaven which said, "You are my beloved Son; in you I am well pleased." (Lk. 3:21–23)

◇

John answered them, saying, "I baptize with water, but there stands one among you whom you do not know. It is he who, coming after me, is preferred before me, whose sandal strap I am not worthy to loose."

These things were done in Bethabara beyond the Jordan, where John was baptizing.

The next day John saw Jesus coming toward him, and said, "Behold! The Lamb of God who takes away the sin of the world! This is he of whom I said, 'After me comes a Man who is preferred before me, for he was before me.' I did not know him; but that he should be revealed to Israel, therefore I came baptizing with water."

And John bore witness, saying, "I saw the Spirit descending from heaven like a dove, and he remained upon him. I did not know him, but he who sent me to baptize with water said to me, 'Upon whom you see the Spirit descending, and remaining on him, this is he who baptizes with the Holy Spirit.' And I have seen and testified that this is the Son of God." (Jn. 1:26–35)

◇

The connection between the Transfiguration and the Baptism of Christ jumps off the page, doesn't it? Did you notice two very similar phrasings: the voice of the Father, which was heard in the Transfiguration and also in the Baptism of Christ, speaking almost identical[8] words: "This is my beloved Son, in whom I am pleased" (Matt. 3:17, Mk. 1:11, and Lk. 3:22). The three Transfiguration narratives repeat this phrase and then add the words "listen to him" (Matt. 17:5, Mk. 9:7, and Lk. 9:35).

The voice of the Father makes both of these events exceptional in all Scripture. This is no small thing: the Father is always difficult to approach and impossible to describe, and although in the Old Testament the voice of God is occasionally heard, this is extremely rare in the New Testament. This rare event shows that there is a deep connection between the Transfiguration and the Baptism of Christ.

In both cases the voice reveals something about the relationship between the Father and the Son, and how the Son reveals the Father to the world. In both events we are given a glimpse of the Trinity, a revelation of what God is, as much as it is possible for us to grasp this. The Baptism and the Transfiguration of Christ are events of divine revelation. The Baptism of Christ is a theophany, a means of revelation of the Godhead, the manifestation of God's glory to the world.

This is a revelation of the entire Trinity. The Baptism of Christ did not merely demonstrate the divinity of Christ to the crowd gathered in Jordan, but it also showed the common activity of Father, the Son, and the Holy Spirit. The Father was made manifest as the one from whom everything else flows. He identified Jesus as the Son, and sent forth the Holy Spirit. The Spirit is made manifest in the image of a dove, an image that was often understood by Christians and pagans as a symbol of spiritual ascent. The Baptism of Christ is one of the rare revelations of the entire Holy Trinity, a revelation of the three persons at once, and a revelation of their respective roles in the salvation of humanity.

If we look carefully at what it is that exactly happens during the Baptism of Christ, we can understand how the three persons of the Trinity operate in relation to each other.[9] The Holy Spirit gives us the guidance, the inspiration, the strength, and the grace to approach God. The way we understand the role and the position of the Holy Spirit within the Holy Trinity, and the way we invite it to form Christ in our lives, is extremely important. The Holy Spirit is God who operates inside us, in our minds and hearts. But salvation is not a lonely road. The full transformation of ourselves starts with God's work inside us, but it is completed when we submit and offer ourselves to him. It is a terrible thought, perhaps, that the presence of Christ in the world depends on us and on our willingness to be his body. But this transition from individuals to members of the body of Christ happens if we accept to offer ourselves. The work is then done by the Holy Spirit of God. The difficult part is to invite the transition and then to step back and allow ourselves to be cleansed and changed.

The Holy Spirit has a distinct origin (the Father) and a distinct destination (the Son). But something else happens before the dove rests in Christ: a revelation of the divinity and the role of Christ in our salvation. The Son, the god-man who acts as a priest, or rather as *the* priest of the universe, unites the divine and the human nature, shown as he steps into the baptism of forgiveness even though the recognized Son of God is sinless himself.[10] The operation of the Holy Spirit reveals Jesus' divinity to bystanders. And it is the Holy Spirit who opens their eyes and ears, affirming Jesus' identification through the words of the Father. Ultimately the Son connects us with the inaccessible God.

What we see here is an outline of the activity of every person of the Trinity toward our salvation. If we could go back in time and see what John the Baptist saw, we would first turn our attention to Jesus: a man, apparently like everyone else, who shows himself to be sinless as he steps up from the River Jordan immediately. But the Holy Spirit, the energy of ascetic ascent, opens our eyes and our ears and we see that Jesus is more than a mere mortal. It is that same Holy Spirit, sent from the Father to make us recognize Christ; the Holy Spirit that then leads us to be baptized with Christ in the Jordan and to be united with him, so that we may with him be called "sons of God" and participate in the eternity of the Father. This is nothing less than the mystery of salvation.

Words cannot say with precision what this mystery means. But the biblical story directs us to reflect on the mystery of the Trinity. First, our attention turns to Jesus Christ, because he brought us the good news and we recognize in him the union of the mortal and the immortal. But reflecting further on Jesus, we discern the operation of the Holy Spirit in the awakening of the spiritual senses, allowing us to discover the mystery of Christ. And finally, we can get a fleeting sense of the Father, the one who expresses the boundlessness and infinity of divinity, to whom Christ is leading us. Even if they are revealed to us by Scripture and tradition, we cannot understand the Trinity fully. But by the fleeting glimpse of the mystery of the Father we know the entire universe is a small and limited bubble next to the eternal and free existence beyond time and space, where God is. There we are given the mystery of the one God in three different ways of being: Father, Son, and Holy Spirit.

As we previously saw, the Transfiguration of Jesus is the other biblical moment where we can see signs of the simultaneous revelation of the Father, the Son, and the Holy Spirit. What might this connection mean?

Both events imply a significant change. There is a distinct connection between the Baptism of Jesus and our own spiritual life, which also starts with a public event of baptism. The rest of our lives are about fulfilling and understanding what happened in that public event. The transition from Baptism toward Transfiguration suggests an internal, mystical path of transformation. What is between our baptism and our spiritual transfiguration in Christ is a life of prayer.

In the same way the Father was manifested in the Baptism of Jesus, he is now manifested in his Transfiguration. And the Father's command to "listen to him" carries a meaning that takes us one step beyond the revelation of the Baptism. Here the words designate Jesus as the living incarnate Word, the reflection and image of the Father.

The difference between the Baptism and the Transfiguration on this point is that while the first was a public event, open for all to see, the latter was an event that took place in front of the three chosen disciples and in front of the Old Testament prophets. The Baptism takes place in front of everyone, and for the benefit of everyone. The Baptism of Christ outlines salvation of humankind as all three persons of the Trinity working together, and thus it *invites* people to the church. Our baptism is the response to the invitation of Christ, and the beginning of our life in him. On the other hand, the Transfiguration of Christ takes place in front of a few people only, followers of Jesus, or those residing with God, according to the biblical expression, "in the bosom of Abraham." The Transfiguration of Jesus demonstrates salvation as it happens mystically, sacramentally, *inside* the church.

Christ's Baptism, Our Baptism

St. Paul adds these three important passages, essential to understanding the meaning of how Christ's Baptism relates to our own journeys with God:

Do you not know that as many of us as were baptized into Christ Jesus were baptized into his death? Therefore we were buried with him through baptism into death, that just as Christ was raised from the dead by the glory of the Father, even so we also should walk in newness of life. For if we have been united together in the likeness of his death, certainly we also shall be in the likeness of his resurrection. (Rom. 6:3–5)

You are all sons of God through faith in Christ Jesus. For as many of you as were baptized into Christ have put on Christ. There is neither Jew nor Greek, there is neither slave nor free, there is neither male nor female; for you are all one in Christ Jesus. (Gal. 3:26–28)

In Him you were also circumcised with the circumcision made without hands, by putting off the body of the sins of the flesh, by the circumcision of Christ, buried with him in baptism, in which you also were raised with him through faith in the working of God, who raised him from the dead. And you, being dead in your trespasses and the uncircumcision of your flesh, he has made alive together with him, having forgiven you all trespasses. (Col. 2:11–13)

And then, consider this, from the Book of Acts:

And he said to them, "Into what then were you baptized?" So they said, "Into John's baptism." Then Paul said, "John indeed baptized with a baptism of repentance, saying to the people that they should believe on him who would come after him, that is, on Christ Jesus."

When they heard this, they were baptized in the name of the Lord Jesus. (Acts 19:3–5)

So what does it all mean for us today? What do the Baptism and the Transfiguration of Christ mean for us today? We have to keep rediscovering their message of salvation. And yet it is not enough to replace the old language with contemporary expressions. The meaning and the context of the biblical and Christ-centered life reveal themselves to us when we approach them as practitioners and participants from the inside. This is something that both the Baptism and the Transfiguration of Jesus still tell us: neither one is related to a moral teaching, or to something that may be said about God in a descriptive way. In fact, very little of what Jesus says or does is *about* God. Very little of what he says or does ever enhances our knowledge of theological matters directly. The work of Jesus—his Baptism and his Transfiguration—is about making God and the kingdom of heaven *present* among us and inside us.

With difficult theological questions like that, I remember how Fr. Zacharias, a simple monk who has lived in the monastery of John the Baptist in Essex for thirty years, would respond when meeting questions, presuppositions, objections, and all sorts of expectations from visiting students.

Fr. Zacharias often talks about the exchange of life between human and God at the chalice of the Eucharist. He talks with reverence and respect, as if this exchange of life is a usual part of his routine: "I bring to the chalice all I can, my entire being, and I prepare for this, and I receive in return the entire life of Christ." He delivers this claim with a humble simplicity that I have seen several times among monks. Despite his age and his long beard, sometimes he looks like a schoolboy who smiles as though he found a coin on the street. People like that give you the sense that they don't know the Bible because they study it; they know it because they live it. And when he looks at the chalice as the source and the center of his life, he thinks of the entire Scripture and tradition as his preparation for the exchange of life. He keeps his mind and his heart in the Baptism of the Jordan River daily, and this gives meaning to his own baptism. He keeps his mind and his heart in the mountain of the Transfiguration, and that transfigures him every day.

Baptism is a powerful thing. According to the Bible, we are to understand our baptism in two different ways: as a rebirth (according to John's Gospel), and as a death and resurrection (according to St. Paul). In the Orthodox tradition we understand this when we watch a baptism rite being performed: the baptized is submerged under the water three times, he or she symbolically dies and is resurrected three times, emerging from the water as a new person, as if born from another womb, this time from the womb of the church, naked, ready to be clothed in white clothes, symbolizing that "as many of you as were baptized into Christ have put on Christ" (Gal. 3:27).

There is something about baptism that suggests that the newly baptized has entered into a different way of being. To say that we recognize Jesus Christ as the Son of God, whose death and Resurrection we share through our membership in his ecclesial body, is not so much a statement of faith as it is an incomprehensible statement that cannot be proven. More than anything else it reflects a leap of faith.

But by identifying ourselves as Christians, we become personally involved in something that touches on, informs, and transforms every aspect of our being. A Christian is someone who is in love with God, who falls deeper into this divine love, and who tries to live every moment in the presence of the divine lover, the God who is known to have only one passion: his strong love for humankind. The confession of faith we make at our baptism is only the beginning of the Christian life, or rather the beginning of a continuous change in Christ.

Something changes in us when we are baptized. The change that happens is a continuous transfiguration that sometimes can be seen by others. Fr. Zacharias from Essex, and many other Christians I have known, look ten to twenty years younger than they are because the love of God radiates from their faces. We know of this also from another source. The tradition of the church speaks of the *good change* of the Christian, which may be seen in the fragrant relics of the saints, centuries after their death. What a mystery this is! Similarly, the Transfiguration of Christ never ceases to be a great mystery—and it presents itself as a fulfillment of the one and only baptism that is confessed in the Creed. What was first revealed to us in the Jordan River has the power to continually transform us.

The Presence of the Holy Spirit

One of the most salient elements in the Transfiguration is the presence and the power of the Holy Spirit. The luminous cloud, the light that shone from the face of Jesus, and even the change in his appearance, were results of the operation of the Holy Spirit. The Holy Spirit always reveals Christ: we read the Bible correctly if we read it in the Holy Spirit. Similarly, we recognize the church as the body of Christ if we are guided by the Holy Spirit. And the complete revelation of the divinity of Jesus Christ on Mount Thabor to Peter, John, and James was also a work of the Holy Spirit.

Although we know the miraculous event on Mount Thabor as the Transfiguration of Christ, there was no change in Christ. What changed was that the Holy Spirit affected the way the three apostles saw their teacher. For the first time they could see his divinity, although he was always God, even when his divinity was hidden. The real change was not in the face or the clothes of Christ, but in the way Peter, John, and James became, by the power of the Holy Spirit, direct participants of the divinity of the Father that was shining to them through Christ.

The mysterious, luminous cloud mentioned in the Gospel narratives suggests the place and presence of God. This cloud recalls the cloud pillar that protected and guided the Israelites through the desert, the dense cloud on the top of Sinai where Moses met God, the cloud that covered the temple of the Lord (1 Kgs. 8:10–12), and countless other instances where the presence of God is understood in specific terms of location.

Yet, the cloud of the Transfiguration remains different than other clouds, because it envelops everyone present. The "place of God" includes Moses, Elijah, Peter, John, and James, along with Jesus. For the first time in history we can understand how the people who make the church become part of the place of God, part of the body of Christ, helping us understand our own incorporation to the body of Christ and our union with him in the church.

The Apocalypse of Peter

The church often read the Transfiguration as an act of Christ who, having "[stretched] out the heavens like a curtain" (Ps. 104:2), now opened it and revealed it to the stunned apostles. In the early church of Palestine, an unusual text called the *Apocalypse of Peter* was read on the Feast of the Transfiguration, a text which does not have the status of Scripture, but was respected as prophetic by many early Christians. The account of the Transfiguration is much longer in the *Apocalypse of Peter* than it is in the canonical Gospels. It is written, supposedly, from the point of view of St. Peter, who describes his amazement at what he sees. Peter asks Christ who the two strange men are that appear in front of them. When Christ identifies them as Moses and Elijah, Peter realizes that a curtain separating this world from the world where Moses and Elijah can be seen in the flesh has been lifted. He proceeds to ask about Abraham, Isaac, Jacob, and all the righteous prophets of the Old Testament. Christ then shows the apostles a fragrant garden, full of trees and fruit. Then "another heaven" opens and the righteous of old are also seen in the flesh.

This fascinating text, widely known in the early church, is interested in what the three apostles saw during the Transfiguration of Christ. While the *Apocalypse of Peter* cannot be taken as historically reliable, it shows us how the Transfiguration was understood among early Christians:

what is revealed here is a different kind of space, one that the text names as "heaven," but not as a limited, definite space. Instead, it implies a different way of existence, one that sees no separation between God and the Creation. The best way we understand this is through Christ himself: wherever he is, is the kingdom of God. The saints, likewise, are in heaven, because they are united to Christ.

In the Baptism narrative the voice of the Father came "from heaven," and in the Transfiguration story the whole otherworldly experience describes heaven, without naming it. The two events are different in this way: in the Baptism of Christ, "heaven" is the place where the Father is. In the Transfiguration the whole scene is taking place in heaven—or at least in the kind of foretaste of the kingdom of God that the three apostles could experience.

In Luke 3:16 an additional biblical connection between the Baptism and the Transfiguration is suggested, where John the Baptist differentiates between the baptism in water that he performs, and baptism in the Holy Spirit and fire that Christ will perform. Although this passage is usually understood in reference to the baptism in the Holy Spirit with the tongues of fire at Pentecost, the Transfiguration can also be said to be such an event: a baptism in the Holy Spirit and in fire, initiated by Christ and administered by the Holy Trinity to the three apostles. Immersion in the Holy Spirit and in the fire that accompanies the Christian life at every step is something we can see on the day of the Pentecost. The mysterious theophany of the Holy Trinity on Mount Thabor, the Baptism, the Resurrection, and the Second Coming of Christ—all these events reveal something about our continuous transfiguration in the Holy Spirit.

Although we may speak of different kinds of baptisms, these are aspects of the same immersion into the power of the Holy Spirit. If we speak of a baptism in water and a baptism in fire, this is so that we can expound on the nature of the one and only baptism that we receive, which includes an aspect of death and rebirth, an aspect of visitation of the Holy Spirit, and also an aspect of becoming immersed in God. But if we see the Transfiguration as "the other baptism," we need to examine the meaning of this phrase a little closer. If it is a baptism, who exactly is baptized? And who is it that baptizes?

The Transfiguration, like all of the biblical events in the life of Christ, was not an event that occurred because Christ needed it. Jesus had no self-serving reason to change the way he looked or the color of his clothes. The event happened for the benefit of those who witnessed it. Rather than being mere spectators, Peter, John, and James were participants in the scene (although Moses and Elijah, who were speaking with Christ and were not overwhelmed by his presence, were even closer to the source of light). The light that shone on them, through the mysterious, luminous cloud and also through Christ, was a light that enveloped them completely, a light that *baptized* them.

We can understand this change of perspective if we consider the rite of baptism. There is a lot of action in a church during a baptism. The priest pours water and blesses. The godparent brings the baby to the baptistery. The parents run left and right, making sure that nothing will go wrong. But the true center of the event is the baby, the little person in the middle of the church who does not do anything. Yet it is for the sake of this little person that the entire event is happening and the Holy Spirit sanctifies the water of baptism. Likewise, when we look at the Transfiguration we think of Christ, his appearance in light, the voice of the Father, and the theological tradition. Yet this event happened for our sake and it is we—the members of the church—that are the focus of this magnificent event.

The Trinity Is Revealed

In the Transfiguration everything becomes clearer, as if the curtain of the mystery has been lifted a little more. Christ shows the way to humanity, as he did in his Baptism, as a priest who speaks for humanity to the Father. This time he also appears as the image of the Father, allowing humanity to see, hear, and experience God directly. Nothing is held back from the vision; the Godhead, the entire Trinity, is revealed fully for the first time in history.

This truth is profound: the curtain hiding heaven was lifted and the Trinity was revealed completely, even if it cannot be seen, understood, or experienced fully. Yet there are some things that we can presume to understand. We understand, for instance, that the Father is heard but not seen, as in the Baptism, and he is not presumed to be "in heaven," since the entire scene takes place in heaven-on-earth. We understand that Christ, in his radiant, glorious form, is shown as the direct and clear image of the Father. We recognize Christ as the mediator between God and humanity, as the High Priest who makes the Father visible.

What is more subtle is the role of the Holy Spirit. In the scene of the Baptism, we see a model of the Trinity where the Holy Spirit is sent from the Father and rests on the Son.[11] But if we turn our attention to the scene of the Transfiguration, we see the Holy Spirit as the grace that awakened the spiritual senses of Peter, John, and James on Mount Thabor, and also as the luminous cloud or the light that dazzled their eyes. But does the light not come also from (or through) Christ? Is the grace the apostles were given not given to them so that they could have the vision of the Transfigured Christ? Was not Christ the one who led the apostles up a high mountain? In all these counts, Christ appears as the cause of the event, playing a role in the outpouring of the Holy Spirit. Therefore, we can see the Transfiguration of Christ as evidence for the double procession of the Holy Spirit, from the Father *and* from the Son.

God revealed himself to us in these three persons because each of them plays a different role in our salvation. Broadly speaking, the role of Christ is to unite divinity and humanity in his person. As the Son of the Father, he is the only one who can address him in our name. At the same time, he is the divine person made visible, and for this reason we start by addressing him. He entered human history when he became one of us, and he is still present among us in a different way, as he offers his body so that the union of the divine and the human can take place on it. The body of Christ is the church, and we are its members. But for this membership to happen, we need to be transformed. This spiritual transformation is the work of the Holy Spirit. The Holy Spirit gives life to the body of Christ, so that it breaks through the limitations of time and space, and it connects the earthly church with heaven. As Fr. Zacharias said, he seeks to lift all the parts of his life and offer them to Christ: the connection of earth and heaven in the church is an exchange of life, the gift of the presence of God to those who dedicate their lives to him.

The Gospel says that "the wind [πνεύμα or Spirit in the Greek text] blows where it wishes" (Jn. 3:8). The Holy Spirit may blow anywhere at all, visit and inspire anyone and at any time, but what happens after the visitation and the direction of its guidance is very specific: it leads to the revelation, recognition, and acceptance of Christ, and the transformation of the individual members into his mystical church body. We can discern whether an act is truly guided by the Holy Spirit because it leads to Christ: but acts that lead to schisms, jealousies, and rivalries are acts that weaken the church and are not guided by the Holy Spirit.

In the case of the Baptism in the Jordan River, we see how the Holy Spirit leads us to Christ: the dove that rested on Christ was seen by the bystanders, by people who had not *yet* constituted the church, but who were called to do so. The next thing that happened was that Andrew, the first-called, recognized Christ (the Messiah) in the person of Jesus, and invited his brother Peter to meet him. The Baptism of Christ in the Jordan and the presence of the Holy Spirit is often seen as the birth of the church.

Showing the Presence of God

In the case of the Transfiguration, Peter, John, and James received the Holy Spirit from the Father, who also identified Christ as his

Son with his words, so that they would recognize Christ as he really was, in his divinity and in his glory. Jesus was the one who invited and guided the three chosen apostles to Mount Thabor. And it was his face and garments that were transfigured in the light of divinity. The light that shone out of his face, which overwhelmed and terrified the apostles, was not the same as the light of the sun, but the light of the Godhead.

Ancient and medieval writers refer to this as the Uncreated Light, the light suggestive of the presence and operation of God. Through this light, which expresses the common activity of the three persons of the Holy Trinity, Jesus was shown to be the radiance of the Father (Heb. 1:3): in his face the unapproachable Father was made manifest. Although the Uncreated Light shone from the Father, who is the principle and the fountain of divinity, it reached Peter, John, and James through the face of Jesus. The Transfiguration shows us that the Holy Spirit can flow from both inside and outside the church. This is something we can see in spiritual life. Many times the preaching and the teaching of the church becomes the vehicle that invites outsiders. Very often we see that the grace of God is extended where the seed of the gospel has fallen. We do not know where, when, or how the Holy Spirit may act, but we know that the Holy Spirit has touched people who were not members of the church, and who did not receive their calling from the church.

What we do know is what happens after the touch of the Holy Spirit. The grace of its touch reveals the intense love of God for humanity, and the person who was given the Holy Spirit seeks the house of this love, and the person who has made it possible for us to be with God. Anyone who is touched by the Holy Spirit, anyone who responds to its touch and revelation, won't rest until they discover Christ and the church. The operation of the Holy Spirit leads to the revelation of Christ.

Through the Baptism and the Transfiguration of Christ, our eyes are opened to two things: First, that while we do not always know where the origin of the Holy Spirit is, we know where it leads. In our prayer and liturgical life this means that the movement of the Holy Spirit leads to life in Christ. Second, these events point out to us that the Holy Spirit is not an agent of necessity but of freedom. This sense of freedom is one of the first steps of tasting eternal life as communion with God, who is not bound by our limitations of time and space.

The church does not exist because we choose to form it. It exists because the Holy Spirit makes it, acting with a will independent of our own. For this reason there is no way for us to predict when, where, or how the Holy Spirit may act. As in our prayer life, where we may find hope in the bottom of despair, many saints have spoken of the dark night of the soul, the terrifying emptying of the self, the painful collapse of our ego. Through the cracks, however, the grace of God finds a way inside us like light shining through a dark prison. Life of prayer is like that sometimes: we may, in repentance, descend into the deepest layers of self-examination, finding ourselves bound by the chains of sin, necessity, and anger, but often a deep descent invites the bright light of the grace of God, loosening the chains.

We can read the Transfiguration as a revelation of the operation of the Trinity in the church. Everyone present at the scene is already part of the church and illuminated by the Holy Spirit. We see the faithful here being mystically transformed into the body of Christ, and the opening of the kingdom of heaven.

The Holy Spirit moves in a circular way: moving from the Father to the members of the church and bringing them toward Christ, helping them to see him as he really is. The Holy Spirit also moves from Christ toward members of the church, revealing to them the Father through the Son. The Transfiguration was a model of deification, where the very body of Christ was being transformed by the Holy Spirit into the body of the church, a body of light that extends and encompasses those who unite with him, and that collapses the limits between the fallen world and heaven. This is how Christ exists in the church, and why, despite our sinfulness, we refer to the church as *holy*. The Transfiguration was a presentation of the mystical and sanctifying work of the church, where we can see the simultaneous operation and participation of the Father, the Son, and the Holy Spirit. To contemplate the Father is to contemplate the mystical source of all life and love, who longs to be with us. To contemplate the Son is to discern how God becomes like us in order for God and humans to meet face to face. To contemplate the Holy Spirit is to awaken the divine touch that waits deeply inside us, for the chance to transform from a life of necessity and pain to a life in Christ. The Transfiguration reveals and outlines the whole mystery of salvation. And his Transfiguration invites us to transfigure with him.

Like the music the nymphs played for the Cretan boy, this revelation is only the beginning for a life that tries to measure up to it. Peter, intoxicated by the light of God, wished to stay on Mount Thabor forever. For the rest of their lives, Peter, John, and James held the vision of the Transfigured Christ. Peter, years after the event, remembered it in his second epistle as "a light that shines in a dark place, until the day dawns and the morning star rises in your hearts" (2 Pet. 1:19). And John mentions it in the beginning of his Gospel, right after he speaks of God as light: "the Word became flesh and dwelt among us, and we beheld his glory, the glory as of the only begotten of the Father, full of grace and truth" (Jn. 1:14). In some way, this vision permeates their witness to Christ until the end.

It is no surprise, then, that according to the tradition of the church, Christ was transfigured in order to prepare his apostles and explain to them the culmination of his ministry and the difficult days of his Passion and Crucifixion that were ahead.

3
HE LED THEM UP A HIGH MOUNTAIN
Following Christ and Crucified with Him

G OING UP A MOUNTAIN IS DIFFICULT; it requires stamina and energy. As we walk or climb toward the top, our body feels that we are asking it to do something out of the ordinary, especially if this is not an exercise we do very often. But in addition to the difficulty and the effort, the landscape around us changes as we proceed higher. The vegetation becomes scarce and eventually stops, the sunlight is more relentless, and the character of the place is defined by rock formations rather than by trees and vegetation. When you reach the top of the mountain, you feel that you came to an end—at least an end in what the earth can give you—and that if you want to go even higher you would have to fly.

I still have a photograph that my father took when I was thirteen years old that reminds me of a very special day. In that photograph I can see myself as I was then, on the top of a mountain, looking up as if I am wondering, "Where else can I go from here?" The photograph was taken on my thirteenth birthday. My father chose to mark the date with a hike on the mountain Erymanthos in the Peloponnese—the same mountain where Hercules had chased and captured the legendary Erymanthian boar. I'm not sure if he chose to take me on a hike because the August weather was particularly inviting that day, or because he wanted to share his love of mountains with me. It took us several hours to reach the peak, and although many years have passed since then, I still remember the feeling of conquering that mountain on that day. It was something like a rite of passage, as if I were leaving behind me the ease of childhood, about to proceed on to the challenges of manhood. I don't know if my father, in his wisdom, had planned for me to have just such an experience, but I remember the great effect it had on me.

This is one of the elements of the Transfiguration narrative that has attracted the interest of writers for many centuries: ascending to the heights. Although the mountain of the Transfiguration was assumed to be Mount Thabor, eleven miles west of the Sea of Galilee, the Gospel narratives do not specify on which mountain the Transfiguration occurred. With an elevation of only 575 meters above sea level, Mount Thabor is actually not very high. But Mark and Matthew refer to the mountain of the Transfiguration as "a high mountain." Luke, strangely, refers to it as simply "the mountain," an expression that sounds as if it is used for a known or previously mentioned peak. However, this can also be understood as referring to any mountain or to whatever mountain was closest to them. (As we might say today, "I am going to the beach.")

Perhaps there is a reason for the reluctance of the evangelists to name the mountain. It is interesting that the location is not specified in any of the canonical or the apocryphal sources, which give many other points of information about the Transfiguration. Although the tone of the Transfiguration narratives is decisively specific regarding the Transfiguration itself, what we read in the biblical narratives about the mountain and the ascent is not described very specifically. We merely read that there was some sort of ascent and some sort of separation from the other apostles, both of which are not really explained. The biblical narrative is more interested in the act of the ascent, as well as in the act of the separation, rather than in the specific site where the event took place.

The Transfiguration is an event with a highly sacramental character, a wondrous manifestation of Jesus as the high priest. In this respect,

Christ, in his glorious appearance in the high mountain is a model for the bishop in the "high place," the throne of a bishop in the altar of a church. Likewise, the separation of Jesus and the three disciples from the rest of the twelve before their ascent to Thabor is reflected in the Eastern tradition's liturgical separation of the priest before he assumes his liturgical duties.[12]

Symbolism of the Mountain

Ascending to the high mountain had several strong precedents in the Old Testament and in the ancient world. Ancient Greek mythology made Olympos, the highest mountain in Greece, the residence of the twelve gods. Mount Helikon, similarly, was the dwelling of the Muses, and Mount Parnassos was where Deucalion and Pyrrha created the humans that populated the earth after the deluge, according to Greek mythology. The Bible is even more connected with mountains of historical and metaphysical importance. Zion, Ararat, Nebo, Thabor, Hermon, Carmel, Olivet, and Calvary are all important and sacred mountains for different reasons. The most important among them are Sinai and Horeb, which may be different names for the same mountain. And the Christian tradition continued this association of spirituality with high mountains, even to our days. Christian monastic "holy mountains" include Mount Athos, but also Monte Cassino, Ganos, Latros, and many others that provided separation from the world to contemplative monks.

There is something about mountains that allowed them to be connected to spirituality and spiritual ascent in popular imagination. The mountain for the Greek world was the equivalent of the Egyptian desert, a place where ascetics could go and separate themselves from the rest of the world. It is for this reason that Greek mountains have an ascetic aura about them. In a wonderful passage on the symbolism of nature in the Bible, St. Maximos the Confessor compared the ascent of a mountain with a spiritual ascent:

Scripture refers to the higher form of the spiritual contemplation of nature as "hill-country" [ὀρεινήν]. Its cultivators are those who have rejected the images derived from sensible objects, and have advanced to a perception of the intelligible essences of these objects through the acquisition of the virtues.[13]

Moses on Sinai

Of all the biblical ascents, the ascent of Moses on Sinai was the most influential. This ascent, which we can find in the book of Exodus, was seen as the greatest model of spiritual life for many centuries. Whether or not it is historically precise in its description in Exodus, the encounter between Moses and God on Sinai, where Moses was given the Ten Commandments in two stone tablets, determined the identity and the future of both Judaism and Christianity.

The first person who described the ascent of Moses on Sinai as a spiritual journey paralleling the spiritual journey toward God was Philo, a Jewish writer who lived around the time of Christ, known by his religion as Philo Judaeus, or by his home city as Philo of Alexandria. Philo did something monumental that would be imitated by many other writers after him, for many centuries. He was the first person to connect the biblical, Hebrew tradition with the Greek philosophy and the scientific worldview of his time. This was, for the most part, the philosophy that has its roots in Plato and Aristotle, but it also included several ideas developed by other philosophical strands, such as the Stoics. In doing so, he expressed the biblical message and Jewish religious concerns in a way that made sense to the wider cultural context of the people who lived in the Roman Empire at the time.

Philo's genius has left its mark on Christianity throughout the world. His combination of biblical tradition with the Greek philosophy prepared the pagan world for the theology of Christianity, and also provided the developing Christian thought with the philosophical vocabulary that would later be indispensible in the formation of doctrine. Some of the fundamental and most interesting concepts of Christian theology were put forth for the first time by Philo. For instance, in his writings, which precede John's Gospel by many decades, he introduced the Logos, the Word, as the most important among all the powers of God. It is impossible to read the beginning of John's Gospel and not think that the concept of God as Logos has something in common with the thought of this Greek Jewish writer. Unfortunately for Philo's fame, the Christian writers who were influenced by him did not credit his name because he was not Christian. His imprint on Jewish scholarship, on the other hand, is not as deep, because it developed along a different path.

The idea of the ascent toward something higher, something more complete and more true, the idea of breaking through the fallen world and approaching God, is something we find in pagan thought before we find it in the Christian ascetic tradition. Philo, as well as other writers who followed him, such as Gregory of Nyssa in the fourth century, and the mysterious and extremely influential writer who wrote under the name of Dionysios the Areopagite in the fifth or sixth century, saw the ascent of Moses on Sinai as a model for an ascetic ascent toward God.

In the book of Exodus we find descriptions of several encounters between God and Moses or between God and the elders of Israel. Chapters 19, 20, 24, 32, and 34 of Exodus tell of some sort of ascent and direct meeting with God. We also see that Moses went through some sort of purification before he started his ascent. We read that on his journey to the top of Sinai Moses saw flashes of light and heard sounds like those made by trumpets. The narrative also notes that the top of Sinai was covered in a thick cloud of darkness, which Moses entered in order to meet God. Finally, in one of the most famous passages of the Old Testament, Moses asked to see God face to face, but his wish was not granted. These basic components of Moses' ascent have a spiritual significance that exceeds the historical context of his climb up Sinai.

A Process of Purification

Christian writers in the early church developed an understanding of the Christian life as a life of constant ascent and struggle along a threefold process of purification, illumination, and union with God. This process was based on the ascent of Moses: the stage of purification (Exod. 19:10–16) has its counterpart in the long and continuous struggle against demons and temptations, as we find it first in the lives of the desert saints, but also in our own lives today. Purification in a deeper sense, as struggle against sin, takes us beyond the understanding of sin as a transgression of a divine or human law. It is not enough to simply obey the Ten Commandments of Moses, the hundreds of other commandments that may be found in Scripture, or the law of the land. Purification in the context of preparing to meet with God is something much deeper, and much more difficult.

To understand purification better, we can turn our attention to the parable of the Pharisee and the tax collector, from Luke chapter 18. The Pharisee standing in the middle of the temple was boasting of his achievements—I fast twice a week, I give one tenth of what I own, I do not rob, I do not do evil, I am not an adulterer. There is no reason to assume that he was not telling the truth. As a Pharisee, a member of a learned and pious group that studied the law of Scripture, he believed that justification comes from obeying the law of God, from obeying literally all the commandments. He was, undeniably, a model of the upright and moral life. Yet the condemnation of Christ is unequivocal. And it was the sinful yet humble tax collector, also praying in the temple at the same time but in a very different way, confessing his sinfulness before God, who went home justified, the Bible tells us.

This parable is more than a commentary on morality. Sometimes when we turn our eyes high hoping to receive comfort and support from God, if our exhaustion or despair has succeeded in displacing our strong self-importance, we may sense something true about our relationship with God, something we can see in the case of the humble tax collector: we talk more clearly to him when we speak in humility, with "a broken spirit" as Psalm 51 puts it (51:17).

I experienced this very phenomenon in a little church whose birth I witnessed. The first few years in the life of this new church most people were busy with study, with practical matters, with catechism, with finding the necessary books, with the appropriate decoration of the church, with performing things in a liturgically precise way, with training singers and servers, and so forth. Three years later, when everything had been put in place and people had relaxed from their first enthusiasm, a time of difficulty set in for the congregation.

As a few of us were gathered to celebrate Vespers, I sensed that we were not concerned with what needed to be done, for the first time since the church had begun. For the first years of its existence, the congregation had acted like Martha in Luke 10:40 who was "distracted with much serving," but there came a time when it could simply sit at the feet of Jesus. The business of the beginning had been valuable. Doing all the practical things was necessary because they trained us, they helped us to address God with our mind, our heart, our vision, our hearing, and all our senses, in such a way that prayer had, finally, become a way of being. And most people were doing these tasks in humility, knowing that we would always be a small church, that our tasks would always be more difficult than we could achieve, that we would always do the best we could, and it would never be quite enough. But in this, the people had learned to pray in humility and to trust, to look inside themselves, to find themselves lacking in strength and virtue, and to offer this lack of virtue to God as a gift, as if saying: "We are poor people, not very smart and not very well-disciplined. We do not have much goodness inside us, we have not managed to go very far in the way of virtue, and everything that has happened here has happened despite our shortcomings, only because it was in your name. We have not been able to achieve anything that we can take credit for, and we do not feel that we deserve any reward for anything. We only hope that you won't treat us according to our mistakes, because we have made many of them. And we know that we'll keep making more mistakes. We do not have anything else to offer you, only our despair and our trust in you. We have shown you everything that is inside us, there is no point in trying to hide from you, so we do not feel any more shame." This, to my mind, describes how the purification of the self can start with an acknowledgment of our true condition rather than with trying to find reasons to be boastful in our spiritual life.

The Second Stage

The stage of illumination is the second stage in the path of Christian asceticism. This corresponds with a very strange passage in Exodus and the ascent to Sinai, which mentions the trumpets heard by Moses and the people of Israel, and the lights Moses saw on his way to the top of the mountain (Exod. 20:18). Perhaps what is most important about this stage is to remember that it is not the beginning and it is not the end, and yet it is where the activity of most well-meaning Christians begins and ends. By illumination we mean everything we could possibly think of as knowledge about God, everything that we have ever known about Christ—his Incarnation, Passion, and Resurrection—everything that we could study about Scripture, the lives of the saints, the doctrines of the church, everything we would ever want to know about Christianity.

Illumination suggests some things. First, it means to dispel the darkness of false belief. Christianity as illumination means the pursuit of truth. Christianity is not a collection of the moral and social codes that we need in order to survive, or a reflection of what we would like to motivate and inspire us. God is not our invention. Likewise, the views, doctrines, and practices of the Christian church try to bring us closer to the Godhead that can describe itself with the words of Exodus 3:14, "I am who I am" (or according to the Greek version of the Old Testament, "I am the one who exists"), and the words of John 14:6, "I am the truth." Christianity therefore does not try to present itself as a better, more convenient religion, or even one that is more consistent with social needs and views, but as the way to a cosmic truth that is not formed by our own ideas, in the same way that the sky is blue whether we believe it or not.

Therefore, from a Christian point of view, idolatry refers to any kind of idea (the word *idolatry* is actually related to the word *idea* etymologically) that tries to replace God—in other words to replace God with the idea of God. Illumination in relation to this sense means to break free from superstition. It is surprising, given the scientific level of modern civilization, how many pre-Christian superstitions still survive in the modern world—zodiac signs, quasi-magical rituals with no theological or empirical basis, good luck charms, belief in reincarnation, and so forth. By the same token, idolatry is an attempt to reduce the understanding of God to something finite, even when it is done under the name of Christianity.

Illumination also means the observation and the interpretation of the created world and its purpose from a Christian perspective. This is something we see in several liturgical services. The service of Vespers, for instance, which begins with Psalm 104 (103 in the Septuagint), the psalm of David that celebrates creation, connects our trust in the continuous support of the world by God with the ancient ritual of the lighting of the lamps. At nightfall, which used to come as a source of great fear to ancient cultures, we celebrate our trust in God and the beginning of the new daily cycle of prayer. The service of Vespers is structured around the prayer of the lighting of the lamps, one of the most ancient hymns of the church, the hymn "Oh, Gladsome Light."

In the night that surrounds us, we place our hope and our trust not in the physical sun, but in the spiritual sun that is Christ, having shone his light in the world. What used to be a time of fear has now become the time of our first celebration of our trust in God.

Finally, illumination suggests our gradual change within the church. This change cannot be measured from the outside. This change, this formation that the church facilitates, is much more deeply situated than at the level of behavior. This is a long process that takes a lifetime of asceticism. According to the experience of monastics who have explored these paths, this formation is a persistent penetration into the inner self, which does not stay at the level of the law but proceeds to the origin of the vices and the virtues inside us. Rather than concentrating in an act of charity, for instance, the focus is on a change at a deeper level inside us, so that we become naturally charitable without having to think about it consciously or making an effort. Yet even if it facilitates such a deep change inside us, illumination does not automatically or necessarily lead to salvation.

Union with God

The final stage of the spiritual ascent toward God is the most dramatic one, according to the accounts of those who saw ascetic ascent as the ascent of Moses. In the final stage of the ascent, Moses "drew near the thick darkness where God was" (Exod. 20:21). This darkness, this dark cloud, suggests that Moses entered a different way of being, as if he were a blind man in the darkness, where his wisdom or intellect did not help him. What happened there, inside the dark cloud? If we remember Exodus 33:18–23—where Moses asks to see God in his glory, but is allowed to see only God's back—Moses spoke with God, but he did not see him. Moses entered the dark cloud and contemplated God. Instead of appearing in front of Moses as another being, as the tradition of the church explains, God united with him in a way that words cannot describe. It is through this union that Moses experienced God: not by turning outward, but by turning inward.

This final stage of the spiritual ascent is that of union with God, and it allows us to put everything else in perspective. The journey toward God according to this model is an inward journey, a pursuit of the "third heaven" beyond time and space. It is also the most elusive part of anything that touches on the study of spirituality, religion, and theology. This stage in the model of ascent essentially means that there is a moment when everything we know about God (or rather everything we think we know), everything we believe (as far as *belief* and *faith* are words that mean something similar to "idea" and "conviction"), everything we can expect, even everything we can hope, becomes irrelevant. Asceticism, purification, the struggle against vices and the encouragement of virtues, our religious education, have served only one purpose: to bring us in front of the presence of God. What happens next? Nothing that words can describe.

The early church borrowed the word *apophatic* from the pagan philosophical tradition in order to express this experience of the presence of God. This fascinating word literally means "the end of words." It is also connected with the word that is used for "decision" (*apophasis*). The implication is clear: we have reached the end of words, thoughts, and deliberations; now we proceed to action, to a decision.

But in relation to apophatic theology and union with God—such as what occurred with Moses on the top of Sinai—this word, which is often used to describe the church, means something more impor-tant and relates to the experience of the presence of God. This is not always obvious in theological writings, where apophatic theology is often translated as "negative theology." The reason the adjective *nega-tive* was used is because if we need to talk about God, we might do it more easily by comparing and contrasting ourselves with what we know of the physical world. This means that God is *not* visible, *not* created, *not* bound by time or space, and so forth. But to stop there, and to simply state that the only thing we know about God is what he is not, is extremely misleading. Our relationship with God does not stop in agnosticism.

The need to use the idea of the apophatic for the highest level of theological thought suggests something much more affirmative. It suggests that although words, thoughts, and knowledge may not be enough to penetrate the dark cloud of the being of God, we *do* have a direct experience of his presence within the church. Whether we refer to the actual Eucharistic body and blood of Christ, to the providence of God, to the way that liturgical symbolism is a shadow of things that are beyond the physical senses, to the discernment of the image of Christ in each other, to the presence and the operation of the Holy Spirit, to the touch of angels, or to an understanding that draws from a deep and dark part of the soul that knows the presence of God as a wholly Other beyond the things we experience, the apophatic and the symbolism of the top of Sinai refer to the presence of God that is strong in our lives despite our inability to talk about him—or perhaps, his presence as it can be found right after the failure of our words, in the space where our minds cannot reach.

There is a story that dates at least as far back as the thirteenth century that illustrates this in a parable. According to this story, St. Augustine was walking by the beach at the time he was trying to write his book on the Trinity. He came across a little child who had dug a hole in the sand. The boy was taking water from the sea with a spoon and pouring it down the hole he had made. St. Augustine watched him for a while, then approached him and asked what he was doing. The boy, very serious, told him that he was trying to empty the sea into that hole. St. Augustine, smiling, told the boy that this was not possible, since the sea is so vast, and the hole was so small. The boy replied that this impossible task was nevertheless easier than what St. Augustine was trying to do, trying to fit the infinite Trinity in his limited human intellect—and with this, the boy vanished from sight.[14]

This story demonstrates something that was known to the early church. The church since its beginning defined itself in the Eucharistic act rather than in words. Instead of embarking on the futile task of developing a complete theoretical system that described everything we know about salvation and the kingdom of God, the church avoided as much as possible what St. Paul called "foolish disputes, genealogies, contentions, and strivings about the law" (Titus 3:9), and tried instead to speak in symbols, in parables, and in rituals. The same is true for the way we address God. We all pray for the mercy of God and his help in our difficulties, individually and collectively. But if we want to address God in the language of sacrifice, of humility, of repentance, and if we want to send our minds and our hearts to the heavenly altar, we cannot hope to achieve anything by merely using words.

An act is something that has its counterpart inside us, and a liturgical act is something in which we participate with all the levels of our understanding. It is for this reason that the church has always used the language of music and sounds, lights and candles, smells, the body, architecture, images, clothes and vestments, the language of sacred space and festal time.

The Ascent of Elijah

In the Greek folk tradition there is an interesting legend that explains why it is usual for a chapel built on the top of a mountain to be dedicated to Prophet Elijah. According to this legend, Elijah had been a sailor who spent most of his life in tempestuous seas facing shipwrecks and other difficulties of life at sea—a life that many Greek families have known for centuries. But eventually he was fed up with a sailor's life and decided to retire to a place that would not remind him of his former life at sea. He left the sea, taking an oar with him, and walked further and further away from the coast. At every town and village where he stopped, he asked the people whether they knew what that wooden object was. The answer was, not surprisingly, "Of course I know. This is an oar." Upon hearing this, Elijah knew that this was not the place for him and he moved on. Finally, he reached a place in a high mountain, miles away from the sea. He asked the people there the same question, but this time the answer was different: "Of course I know. It is what the baker uses to put bread in and out of the oven." Elijah then, the legend says, decided to make this high mountain his home, and since then churches with his name are found in mountains.

Although this is a lovely story, it does not have much in common with Elijah as we know him from the Old Testament. Elijah is primarily remembered for his ascent to heaven on a chariot and horses of fire, which was witnessed by his disciple Elisha (2 Kgs. 2). This scene is seen frequently in iconography. His flight toward heaven is perhaps reminiscent of the ascent of a mountain, the closest we can climb "up" without a chariot.

Two more convincing explanations are available for the association of Elijah with mountaintops: the first has to do with the name of Elijah as it is given in the Septuagint (Ηλιού) or in its more hellenized form (Ηλίας), which sounds very similar to the Greek word for the sun (ήλιος). We can understand this association when we juxtapose Elijah's ascent with the figure of the sun god as he appears in Greek mythology—a figure who rides his chariot, drawn by wondrous horses, every day in the sky. The cultural meeting of the biblical and the Greek tradition, and also the iconographic renditions of the two scenes, brought these two figures very close to each other.

But we might also note that Elijah, perhaps precisely because of his association with the sun god, is virtually the only character of the Old Testament whose cult was continued in the Greek tradition—a fate not shared by Moses, David, or Isaiah. Even if all the righteous and the prophets of the Old Testament are venerated as saints in the church, it is rare to find churches dedicated to any of them except Elijah. The churches and the icons that depict him in the Orthodox tradition are innumerable. Elijah personified the tradition of ascent not only in theology, but also in the folk tradition.

Nevertheless, the more theologically accurate reason for the association of Elijah and mountain is his ascent to Mount Horeb; he is the only person in the Bible except Moses who is mentioned in relation to this mountain. As we can read in 1 Kings 19, Elijah repeats the journey of Moses in a shorter scale (it takes him forty days to reach his destination, which echoes the forty years of the Israelites in the desert), ascending the same mountain.[15] Elijah wishes to see God as Moses did, but God's response is similar to the one he gave to Moses. In the narrative in 1 Kings 19:9–13, God shows Elijah how to look for him. God was not in the strong wind, the earthquake, or the fire that passed before Elijah, but in a still, small voice. And then, when he realizes where God is, Elijah covers his eyes with his mantle before he goes out to speak with God, similar to how Moses covered himself when God passed in front of him in Exodus 33.

Elijah's narrative of ascent was not as celebrated as that of Moses, and yet his legacy among the Hebrews and the Christians was very strong. While Moses became known as the lawgiver, Elijah was seen as the exemplar of prophecy. The Christian Fathers who interpret the biblical narrative of the Transfiguration see in the presence of Moses and Elijah a symbolic representation of the Law and the Prophets—the two parts that comprise the Old Testament and Hebrew theology.

The ascent of Elijah demonstrates even more clearly than the ascent of Moses the apophatic approach toward God. In the narrative in 1 Kings 19:11–13 we hear first of all the places or events where God is not found before we are introduced to the still, small voice of God. And even then, Elijah has to cover his eyes with his mantle before he speaks with God.

Elijah is repeating the journey of Moses, and many of the elements of his story are similar. The emphasis is different, however. Some things anticipate the experience of Christian asceticism, which naturally saw Elijah as one of its inspirations. Elijah is completely abandoned to the will of God. His journey really starts in 1 Kings 19:4, when he confesses that he is no better than those who preceded him, and therefore he has failed as much as they did. With this, he acknowledges his sinfulness, he wishes to die, and he offers his life to God. From then on he is completely in the hands of God, who sends an angel to feed him and instruct him to go to Mount Horeb.

The journey of Elijah is more inward than that of Moses. Asceticism here maintains the symbolism of the mountain ascent, but is also connected with a withdrawal from the world and an abandonment, or rather, a certain trust in God very similar to what we find a few centuries later in the Desert Fathers.

The Mountain of the Transfiguration

The ascetic tradition had always been interested in models of spiritual ascent. In the first few centuries most of the Eastern Christian writings on spiritual ascent used almost exclusively the model of Moses ascending Sinai, but sometime after the seventh century something changed. Christian ascetic writers realized that while the ascent of Moses and Elijah did not reach its end in the Old Testament, their zeal to see God face to face and to speak with him was fulfilled at the Transfiguration of Christ.

God revealed himself only gradually to Moses, through three successive encounters. The first encounter took place at the burning bush, when Moses wished to learn the name of God. The answer "I am who I am" (as is given in most English translations) or "I am the one who exists" (which is what we get if we translate the Greek version of Exodus) or "I was and I am who I will always be" (which is an attempt at a more literal translation of the Hebrew text) is only a partial one. At the same time this answer reveals something about the eternal nature of God, it also implies that it is difficult to address him face to face. In addition, since knowledge of a name suggests knowledge of what this name signifies, the answer of God at the burning bush implies that it is not possible for Moses, a mere human, to know God.

The second stage of the revelation of God is when Moses is given the law on Sinai. This contact was more extensive, and it led to the formation of the people of God. Even then, however, God refused to show himself to Moses—something that Elijah later is fully aware of, since he covers his face with his mantle before he talks to God. Therefore, this encounter, as well as the meeting of God and Elijah, did not end in a full revelation of God. The gap between God and humanity was still too great.

The third stage of this revelation took place on Mount Thabor, when it was finally possible for Moses and Elijah to see God face to face, talk with him, and know him as much as was possible. This time God reveals to them his name, which is possible to do through Christ. The name by which we address God, which allows us to unite with him, is the Father of Jesus Christ. Through our incorporation to the body of Christ, we address God as Christ taught us in the Lord's Prayer: our Father.

For all these reasons, the model of spiritual ascent that the early church expressed in the ascent of Moses was replaced by the model of the spiritual ascent and revelation that took place on Mount Thabor. The symbolism of Sinai gradually receded after the seventh century, and when theologians write about the mountain that leads to God, they mean Thabor, the mountain of the Transfiguration.

Following Christ

The revelation of God is not a matter of knowledge but a matter of love. In the light of Mount Thabor, the divinity of Christ was revealed completely to Peter, John, and James, but they were still not able to take in all the might of the presence of the divinity and they fell to the ground in terror, as blinded by the excessive light. By the end of the event, it is hard to say whether the three disciples of Christ had learned something more about the nature of God. And yet, they had a very strong experience of his presence that made words redundant.

The experience of Peter, John, and James was similar to the experience of Paul on the way to Damascus (Acts 9; 2 Cor. 12) who, without warning, was taken up to the kingdom of God. In both cases we see a reluctance to describe in words what they experienced. Paul says that "he was caught up into Paradise and heard inexpressible words; which it is not lawful for a man to utter" (2 Cor. 12:4), meaning that it was not possible to translate into words what he saw and what he heard. Peter, John, and James, on the other hand, were instructed directly by Christ to keep the event to themselves until after his Resurrection (Mk. 9:9; Matt. 17:9; Lk. 9:36). Both these cases remind us of the apophatic as an expression of the reality that, while beyond words, may still be experienced.

The dynamic relationship between God and humanity has always started with something that God does. In the case of the Transfiguration, Peter, John, and James were called by Christ and ascended the mountain with him. In this case, as well as in the cases of Moses and Elijah, all these people were called or guided by God first, but that was not enough. They had to ascend the mountain.

The experience of many ascetics and writers, as well as the experience of many Christians, is that there is some sort of collaboration between God and humanity for our salvation, that although God provides opportunity after opportunity and keeps calling us toward him, it is up to us to accept the invitation of God, and to look for him in the mountain of asceticism. And yet, in a strange way, although we need to put a lot of effort and energy toward this goal, the illuminated mind that ascends to the top of the mountain cries, as Augustine did, that it is all God, from beginning to end.

Nevertheless, although Augustine's emotional exclamation speaks the truth at a different level, the complete picture includes the mountain of asceticism as well as the grace of God. What makes the difference is that although we often think of the ascetic ascent as the cultivation of virtues and the fight against passions that can transform us, this transformation is not so much a struggle to prove ourselves, or to create our own salvation, as it is a way to train ourselves to be better divine lovers. The way to salvation is like a courtship with God. We don't need to justify ourselves in the eyes of our beloved, and sometimes we don't even care if we are loved—but as an act of love we want to make space inside us so that we live and breathe the beloved, and we dedicate our time and energy to them. The way to salvation is an act of irrational, selfless love.

We often describe God with adjectives that exalt his greatness, such as *all-knowing* and *everywhere present.* We also call him all-powerful or omnipotent. Yet we may be trapped by our own conceptions into holding a false image of God. God may be beyond time and space, and he may be beyond the reach of natural laws, but he is not literally omnipotent. There is one thing that he cannot do. God is incapable of existing in any other way except in the way of love. His way of acting is the way of love, and this is something we see throughout the Christian narrative—from the Creation of the world to the Crucifixion, the ultimate act of self-sacrifice. In his desire for us God covered the distance between him and us and became mortal so that he could make it possible for us to exist in a union with him.

Our salvation depends on if we will look at God and recognize him as the Bridegroom, as the mad lover of humankind, and if we will be moved by his love and respond in the same way. Salvation is not a hope to receive a not guilty verdict from a terrible judge who knows every dark secret of our life; it is a union of love between our mortal nature and God, a divine wedding. And asceticism, as we find it in the early Christian tradition, is the training of our heart, mind, and body so that we can synchronize with God at every level of our existence and trust ourselves to him. If we look at our relationship with God in this way, we have already invited him to lead us to him.

Why is it difficult for us to practice this complete trust of our life to God? It often seems like a limitation of our freedom. And yet, freedom of choice and free will certainly have their place in the work of salvation. The first exercise of human freedom was Adam and Eve's decline of God's offer of salvation, eternal life, and communion with him. Nevertheless, it is important not to think of the Fall as a historical event that happened to two people who have nothing to do with us. While Adam and Eve could not predict the results of their actions, we certainly can, and yet we also continuously decline the free and unconditional offer of salvation and eternal life. Our fall is a present reality, not a historical memory. And yet, it is only with fall, damnation, and death as real options (surprisingly difficult to resist!) that any choice at all is meaningful: if free will played no role, and if salvation or damnation did not depend on our choice, our destiny would be nothing more than mechanistic determinism. We would not be responsible for our choices and our sins. Worst of all, we would not be able to see God as lover.

On the other hand, the saints who submitted their lives to the hands of God tell us that the actual work of salvation, the actual union of our created nature and the uncreated God, is not something they can take credit for as a result of their own acts. Some of them saw the presence of God at every stage and cried that their way toward God was all grace, from the beginning to the end, from the very first signs of revelation or stirring of the consciousness, and all they had to do was to give themselves to God, without any thoughts of justification or salvation. As Peter said in the presence of the Transfigured Christ, "It is good for us to be here."

In the Transfiguration narrative we have the three apostles who were called by Christ and who responded to his call, who experienced all the difficulties of the ascent to a high mountain, but who were never left alone by Christ in their ascent. It may be true that the ascent of the apostles to the top of Mount Thabor corresponds with the ascetic ascent in our lives, because Christ calls and the Holy Spirit gives the strength and the grace, but it couldn't happen without the acquiescence of the apostles—and it cannot happen without our acceptance. The ascent on Thabor, as the ascent toward salvation, is certainly a work of freedom.

Holy Freedom

Freedom is an elusive concept. The secular understanding of freedom, which is safeguarded by our democratic society, is the freedom to choose among several options, the ability to deliberate, to consider possibilities, to measure our strength and to choose a course of action. But at the level of divine love, freedom means something completely different. A person who is good does not consider evil. More important, a person who is in love does not consider separation from the beloved as an option. For God, who is both good and loves humanity without limits, freedom does not mean the option to step away from and abandon his creature, but to act in the most irrational way if it can bring about even a chance of bringing that creature closer to him. And what is the voluntary Incarnation and Crucifixion of God, if not the most irrational act in the entire history of the universe? The death of Christ on the cross is an act of God's passionate love for humankind, and for this reason it shows that God is free, above any necessity. When we crucify the self on the Cross of Christ, we respond to his Crucifixion by placing our love for God above necessity and rationality, and in this way we participate in the freedom of God.

For the person who has felt the love of God, even at a small scale, freedom as deliberation and choice among many options does not make any sense anymore. God is the most intense, the most manic lover of humankind, and the person who feels this love, even at its most difficult expression, sees as his only freedom not the deliberation but the action of responding to this love. In exactly the same way that an infatuated lover has no option but to use all his energy trying to remove whatever separates him from his beloved, the person who responds to the love of Christ once he has felt it understands freedom in this transfigured way. This freedom is the freedom to follow Christ on the way to the mountain—Thabor or Calvary. It is in this way that we can think of this ascent as an ascetic ascent in full freedom.

There is something subtle in the way we understand this ascent as an ascent of love: the call of God and the experience of the love of Christ precede the ascent to the mountain. We find this in a different way in the story of Moses, whose ascent is a solitary one, but here too the call of God and his partial revelation in the burning bush has taken place before the ascent. The Transfiguration narrative, on the other hand, builds on the initial confession of faith, or rather of trust, that precedes the ascent (the confession of Peter that Christ is the Son of God). It also builds on the promise of the Passion and the Resurrection, and also on the promise of the kingdom of heaven, that are given to the disciples of the Word. These words seduced the disciples. The presence of Jesus among them, which led to their increasing realization that he is the Son of God, as we see in the narrative that immediately precedes the Transfiguration passage, also gave them an initial, if incomplete, experience of the love of God. After this, every step they took with him brought them even closer to him and his love. As the biblical narrative presents it, they did not just follow Christ in the ascent to the high mountain; he actively took them and led them to the high mountain. This action sounds like the action of the one who initiates the relationship.

Following the Church

How does this apply to us, outside the strict historical context of the ministry of Christ? How can we claim to have the experience of Christ in the present age, two thousand years after he ascended to heaven? Nothing has really changed. In some ways it is even easier for us because the apostles were being given an unprecedented revelation whose magnitude far exceeded anything they could possibly anticipate, a revelation that was far above the messianic hopes of Judaism. For this reason their knowledge was working against them, it was telling them that what was happening to them was impossible. We, on the other hand, know about the Incarnation, the Passion, the Resurrection, the ministry, and the Transfiguration of Christ. We also know that even after his Ascension the Holy Spirit has remained continuously present in the church. Though he is not present in the same sense as when Andrew and Peter looked his face, Christ is as present now among us as he was when he was travelling to Capernaum and to Caesarea Philippi with his disciples.

Perhaps it is even less difficult or less scandalous to recognize God in the church than it was to do so in a human being. To be sure, we cannot imagine the people in the market of Jerusalem or Nazareth noticing Jesus walking and then turning to each other saying, "Oh, the Son of God just walked by." We may think it is difficult for us to hold fast to our faith, since the historical presence of Christ on earth took place two thousand years ago, and therefore we may have missed something of its immediacy. Yet this must have been even more difficult for the people who lived at the time of Christ, for whom it was an even greater challenge to accept that the almighty God had become the unassuming thirty-year-old who was in front of them. It was both a gradual revelation given to them, exactly as it was given to Peter, John, and James on Mount Thabor, and a realization that this human being was actually the fulfillment and the center of the texts and prophecies that their tradition held as sacred for centuries. It is much easier for us to approach what Christ is now, even at an initial level, and to recognize his presence in the church.

At the same time, the church as a continuous manifestation of the presence and the miracle of Christ includes everything that was made manifest in the historical Incarnation. The Transfiguration is an event that keeps happening. The disciples (we) are still led by Christ in the mountain of asceticism, after they come to know him. That ascent never ends, but the continuous Transfiguration this time takes place in the people who bear Christ inside them. The light that shone on Mount Thabor keeps shining throughout the centuries and the generations, as a living memory. But, following the example where the presence precedes the ascent, the church does not operate primarily as a teaching center, although teaching is part of what it does.

In a way, the role of the church and all Christians is to save inside them and manifest the image and the presence of Christ and the kingdom of God on earth. Everything else that is connected with Christianity, such as good works, charity, and even faith and love, flows from the presence of Christ, and eventually is important only inasmuch as it leads us toward Christ. Before anything else, we start with what makes Christ present among us—the liturgical life of the church. It is because of the sacramental presence of Christ in the church that we can say that Christ is present with us in the here and now.

The liturgical act speaks volumes even to people who have not had any prior exposure to Christian theology or tradition. One of the stories that Orthodox Christians like to remember is the story of the envoys of the Russian leader in the eleventh century who were sent to different parts of the world and inquired about their religion. At that time the Russians, or Rus, were coming in contact with the Christian world, and their prince considered the adoption of Christianity for his subjects. The question was which version of Christianity he should adopt, if he were to go ahead with this plan.

So he sent envoys to several parts of the Christian world to observe how Christianity was practiced there, and asked them to submit their reports to him. Naturally, the prince and the envoys examined as many aspects of the religious life of the places they visited as possible. What tipped the balance in favor of Greek Christianity was the fact that its liturgical life revealed the touch of God in the eyes of the Russians. The envoys who were sent to Constantinople were taken to the great church of St. Sophia during the liturgy, and experienced something there that caught them completely by surprise. When they returned to Kiev, the old capital of the Rus, they submitted the most dramatic report to their leader: "We did not know whether we were in heaven or on earth, for surely there is no such splendour or beauty anywhere upon earth. We only know that God dwells there among people." Shortly after this, Prince Vladimir was baptized by the Greek Roman emperor, and his people followed him.

What this historical example shows is that the liturgical experience of God can be a starting point for a lifetime of conversion. We often think of the experience of God or the kingdom of heaven as something that may be given at the end of the Christian struggle, as a reward. This is true to some extent, in that the second Jerusalem that the book of Revelation describes, the kingdom of God as we understand it in the gospel, is something that has not fully come yet. On the other hand, it is something we have tasted, even if not completely, after the Incarnation of Christ, since the body of Christ is continuously formed in the church by the Holy Spirit. But in many things we do not start anything on our own but merely respond to something that God has already done for us and toward us—as was the guidance of God to Abraham or Moses, and as was the call of the apostles, so is our response to the call of the church.

Virtue and Purification

There is one more element that is common to the ascent of Moses on Sinai and to the ascent to the mountain of the Transfiguration. In both cases there is a separation of the people who make the ascent from everyone else. In the case of Moses this element is stressed even more, and it is underlined by a process of purification that he undergoes before he starts his ascent. In the Transfiguration narrative we do not find this element of purification, but there is some sort of preparation for the journey in the passages that precede the ascent, as Jesus tells his disciples about his forthcoming Passion and Resurrection, and then, as he addresses them as well as the crowd, he invites everyone who wishes to follow him to deny his own self and to carry his cross with him.

Both the purification of Moses and the purification by the Cross, if we can call it that, are very important. But as often happens in the New Testament, a theme that is first found in the Law and the Prophets is revealed to have a more specifically Christological meaning. Though the purification of Moses is the basis for the ritual purification of priests before they celebrate the Eucharist, through the Christological filter we can view it not so much as a moral purification, but as a preparation for a meeting with God.

But in addition to the purification and the preparation, the separation of Moses or of the three apostles has a priestly character. All of them experienced something that was beyond their ability to comprehend. The preparations that Moses undertook and the silence Christ asked of his disciples after the Transfiguration both point to the fact that what they experienced is something that may be shared by the people who have had the initiation to the church mysteries. Moses is often seen as the prototype of the bishop or the priest. Instead of entering a dark cloud, the bishop or priest enters the sanctuary in order to bring back to the people the word of God. The three apostles, in an even more intensely priestly role, accompany Christ on his ascent and are similarly enveloped by a cloud, which this time is not dark but brilliant. They are given the full view of Christ in his divinity and the kingdom of heaven. Despite their fear and trembling, they are later commanded to impart the presence of Christ to the world. This separation is always a necessary part of the priestly ministry, not because it is any indication about the privileged status of the priest but because it shows that the vertical mission of the church, that is, the thrust toward God, is as much a necessary part of the work of salvation as the horizontal mission of the church, that is the gathering and the unity of the believers. This is exemplified in the role of the priest, who expresses with his presence the vertical ascent for and on behalf of the people of God.

What the purification and the separation mean for the world is said plainly by Christ in the passages before the ascent: "Whoever desires to come after me, let him deny himself, and take up his cross, and follow me. For whoever desires to save his life will lose it, but whoever loses his life for my sake and the gospel's will save it" (Mk. 8:34–35). Instead of a solitary and difficult struggle toward justification or morality, Christ asks for something even more difficult—to turn over our life to him. The purification of the self in terms of morality but also in terms of restoring the fallen human nature, is something that follows after this act, and not before. As one of the most respected saints of the church, St. Maximos the Confessor wrote, "It is not virtue that leads to the Truth [Christ], but the Truth that leads to virtue."

For this reason it is better to think of the continuous ascent and Transfiguration within the church as a process inextricably connected with the liturgical and sacramental life of the church. But this is exactly where we can remember the "turn" in St. Paul's letter to the Romans, where he shifted the focus from the historical Transfiguration of Christ to the Transfiguration of the faithful into the body of Christ, as we discussed in the first chapter. The church, as the people of Christ, is led to the spiritual ascent by Christ himself, in exactly the same way Peter,

John, and James were led to the mountain of the Transfiguration by him. The ascent to the high mountain for us is our own response to the word of God, and the trust and faith in which we may accept him. The ascetic mountain for us is the ascent on the way of this trust in Christ and in his Eucharistic body. It is in him, in his revelation and his imparting of his own nature to us, as it happened on Mount Thabor and still happens in the church, that our nature is restored in him. For the love of God.

4

YOU SHOWED YOUR DISCIPLES YOUR GLORY AS MUCH AS THEY COULD BEAR IT

The Anatomy of a Miracle

O NE OF THE WAYS TO APPROACH the Transfiguration of Christ is to consider it as one of the several miracles that Christ performed in order to glorify the name of God, to demonstrate his power, and to offer proof of his divinity. From this point of view the Transfiguration is comparable to biblical events such as the resurrection of Lazarus or the resurrection of the daughter of Jairus, the healing of the ten lepers, the healing of the paralytic, the healing of the blind man, and others.

Over thirty such miracles are mentioned in the New Testament, although Jesus performed many more. As we read in Matthew 15:30–31 for instance, "Great multitudes came to him, having with them the lame, blind, mute, maimed, and many others; and they laid them down at Jesus' feet, and he healed them. So the multitude marveled when they saw the mute speaking, the maimed made whole, the lame walking, and the blind seeing; and they glorified the God of Israel."

Scripture offers some explanations as to why Jesus performed these miracles. In John 14:10–13 we read that Jesus pointed to the miracles as evidence for his divinity and his mutual indwelling with the Father. Yet the Transfiguration of Christ is an event that reveals, among several other things, something about the way God uses miracles, something about the way we relate to them, and something about their significance and their position within the church. But in order to penetrate these mysteries as much as this is possible, we have to examine something about miracles in general first.

Very often the miracles that Christ performed are narrated in such a way that they reveal something about himself and his work of salvation. We can consider, for instance, the specific way Jesus healed the man in John 9 who was born blind. The eyes of this man were not simply healed, but created by clay that Jesus made there, by spitting on the ground. The narrative here offers us an image reminiscent of the original creation of man by God in the book of Genesis. In the Genesis narrative, exactly as in John's Gospel, God creates man using mud and clay that he has molded with his own hands. In performing the miracle in this same way, Jesus revealed that he was one with the one who created the world, or as the Creed says, referring to Jesus Christ, "through whom all things were made." In this act Jesus revealed that he is God before the ages, as much involved with the original creation of humanity as he is with its salvation. This "addition" to the Genesis narrative also allows us to see the relationship between Creation and Christ, and Christ's "cosmic" significance. In other words, as is the case in the majority of the Old Testament references that we find in the Gospels, we are encouraged to read the Old Testament through the prism of the New Testament, and see how the Old Testament prepared humanity for the coming, the ministry, the Passion, and the Resurrection of Jesus Christ.

In addition, that miracle, which Jesus himself tells us had to happen "so that the works of God should be revealed in this man," is connected with one of the most important themes in John's Gospel: the theme of light. Consistent with this theme, the narrative of the healing makes a distinction between natural light and Jesus as the light of the world.

But although we can analyse this miraculous healing even further, and delve into other miracle narratives in a similar way, there is an interesting problem in the Bible. There is no description about the greatest miracle of them all: the Resurrection of Jesus Christ.

This is certainly a challenging problem for biblical criticism, and there are several possible explanations for it. The first that might occur to us is that the Resurrection of Christ is not described in any of the Gospels because there was nobody present to witness it—but this explanation has to be dismissed without second thought. Both the New Testament and the Old Testament contain many passages describing events that were not witnessed by any human. Who heard the prayer of Christ in Gethsemane for instance, since Peter, John, and James were asleep? Who witnessed and transcribed the attempts of Satan to tempt Christ in the desert? Finally, who witnessed the scene in the beginning of the book of Job, where God and Satan talk about Job in the heavenly court? But if we have knowledge of such events it is because it was either given to prophets and saints by the Holy Spirit, or because Christ himself related them to his apostles, and the case of the Resurrection cannot be different. If we envision the first time Jesus appeared to his disciples after his Resurrection, we can be certain that after the initial shock, after the joy, and after the realization that "he is truly the Son of God," they asked him "Master, what happened after we laid you in the grave? Tell us everything and do not skip the smallest detail."

We can see repeatedly, however, that the gospel is not a biography in the sense we would understand the genre today. We can always find a deeper point, a more spiritual reading within, whether as a fulfillment of an Old Testament prophecy, as a prefiguration of the kingdom of heaven, or as something else that is nevertheless relevant to our salvation. The biblical narratives emerged within the context of people who knew the basic facts and were developing their liturgical and prayer life around them. So why was the description of the Resurrection left out, this event second to none in the entire Bible?

An intentional omission expresses a certain difficulty with all miracles. Although the miracles of Christ are performed within a specific context, usually demonstrating a particular point of his divinity or his relationship with the Father, the concept of the miracle in general (at least the miracle as we usually define it, in terms of an act or an event that breaches the laws of nature) touches on something that does not sit well with Christian thought. A miracle is a blatant manifestation of a reality that does not leave room for doubt. For the same reason, it does not leave much room for choice and for free will. When confronted with a miracle, we have no choice but to believe what our eyes and our ears tell us—even if, in defiance of this logic, many people at the time of Christ saw his miracles and yet did not believe in him. If I see the heavens open and Christ appear in front of me in glory, surrounded by clouds and angels, I'll have no option but to believe in him. This, however, is not the way of the church.

While the very existence of the gospel and the church is a continuous testimony to the miracle of the Resurrection of Christ; both the "good news" that the gospel is and the manifestation of the resurrected body of Christ that the church is flow out of his Resurrection. At the same time, this reluctance to include the description of this central event in the Bible anticipates, perhaps, a leap of faith from the ones who receive the biblical word. Instead of being given precise historical details as to how the stone in front of the tomb was removed, how the heart of the dead body started beating again, or what the soldiers who were guarding the tomb saw and how they reacted, the gap in the narrative invites Christians to place themselves there, to accept or not to accept the Resurrection and the presence of Christ freely, without coercion from the text.

The Centrality of the Resurrection to the Life of the Church

The Resurrection of Christ was not celebrated primarily as a historical event among early Christians, or even as a miracle, but as something larger. The Resurrection was the very center of the liturgical life and the worship of the early Christian communities. For the early church, the most naturally occurring understanding about what is in the Eucharistic chalice was that it was nothing else but the resurrected body of Christ. The Resurrection, in other words, was not so much an event that happened a certain time ago, which was concluded then, but was the continuous Resurrection of Christ in the church and the continuous Resurrection of the church in Christ.

One way to look at this is to consider the icon that the Orthodox Church uses for the Feast of the Resurrection. This type of icon presents Jesus clothed in white garments, stepping on the broken gates of Hades (the underworld) under which we sometimes see death personified as a person bound in chains. Jesus reaches to Adam, sometimes also to Eve, and he raises them from their tombs, while on his left and his right we can see other persons from the Old Testament, such as Solomon, David, and John the Baptist (considered by the tradition of the church as the connection between the Old Testament and the New Testament). Although this icon is associated with the Resurrection of Christ, its proper title is *Descent to Hades* (Η εις 'Αδου Κάθοδος).

This icon, which the Eastern Church thought more appropriate for the celebration of Easter than the icon that represents Jesus emerging from the tomb while the soldiers fall to the ground in terror, does not depict the Resurrection of Jesus at all, and has very dubious biblical roots. Chapter 3 of 1 Peter makes a reference to Christ "[preaching] to the spirits in prison" (3:19), but this is the most we can find in the canonical Scriptures that may support the presence of Christ in the underworld. Based on this reference from 1 Peter, a tradition holds that Christ spent three days in the underworld, freeing the dead, before his Resurrection.

On the other hand, the phrase, "Father, into Your hands I commit My spirit," which Christ said on the cross at the moment of his death according to Luke's Gospel (23:46) is also a verse from a Psalm (31:5) that shows trust in God and also suggests that Christ was with the Father immediately after his death. The latter view is more respectable, based on canonical Scripture. The scene of Christ in Hades was inspired by a fourth-century apocryphal writing, known as *Acta Pilati* or the *Gospel of Nicodemus*, which narrates the events surrounding the Resurrection of Christ from the point of view of the dead who were raised when Christ died on the Cross—as it was attested in Matthew 27:52–53.

It is obvious that we would run into all sorts of theological problems if we tried to conceive of the preaching of Christ to the dead, to the "spirits in prison" in historical terms, as an event that happened between his death on the cross and his Resurrection. And yet, the Orthodox Church chose to celebrate Easter with this icon, rather than with the more historically correct image of Jesus emerging from the tomb. The latter image was known in the East since at least the ninth century, but nevertheless it was abandoned in favor of the *Descent to Hades*. Why is this?

The main explanation is that the *Descent to Hades* takes the same distance from the Resurrection narrative that the Gospel does, and most likely for the same reasons. But what is fascinating in considering the icon is that when we juxtapose it to the text, we realize how that missing narrative was understood in the early church when the Gospel was being formed. The action depicted is Christ raising Adam and Eve from the dead, and through them he resurrects the entire human race. This resurrection takes place outside time; it is happening once and always.

Adam and Eve, the ancestors who fell and through their fall tainted the entire world, represent human nature, which was created by God and was raised again after its fall by God. When we see the famous fresco of the *Descent to Hades* in the apse of the monastery of Chora in Constantinople, which places the Resurrection of Christ, or rather the resurrected body of Christ, just above the altar table, we realize that the feast of the Resurrection is not limited to the historical event of the resurrection of Jesus Christ in Jerusalem, in the middle of the Jewish month of Nissan in the years of the reign of Pontius Pilate and Emperor Claudius. Rather, it is extended to the celebration of the Resurrected and Eucharistic body of Christ, around which the faithful defined themselves as Christians, and as the Body of Christ, which is understood as the church. The miracle of the Resurrection, therefore, is something that starts with the bodily Resurrection of Jesus Christ and is concluded with the resurrection of the body of the faithful by him, and the granting of eternal life. This wider understanding of the Resurrection is supported by history but not limited by it.

When we consider the significance of the Resurrection of Christ, we realize that it touches the entire church collectively, and every faithful believer individually. The leap of faith that is needed in order to accept the event of the Resurrection of Christ, which is consistent with the reluctance of the Gospels to describe it precisely, makes it an event that requires our own participation in order to be complete. If this is the case, do we also participate with every miracle in the life and the tradition of Christianity?

Understanding Miracles

What do we mean when we say *miracle*? How does the church understand miracles? Even if we set aside the direct supernatural acts of God, such as the creation of the earth, the planets, the animals, and even the creation of humanity, there are many other miracles in the Old Testament, performed by prophets and people to whom God has granted that power for a reason. We can recall, for instance, the miracles Aaron performed in front of the Egyptian pharaoh, the ten miraculous "wounds" that convinced Pharaoh to allow the Hebrews to leave Egypt; the miracles of Elijah, when he demonstrated the power of God over the priests of Baal; and also miracles such as the protection of Daniel in the den of lions and the protection of the three children that were thrown in the furnace. We can also recall miracles by which the Israelites were sustained, such as the manna from heaven and the rock in the desert from which fresh water sprang.

Miracles are known to other ancient civilizations, in a way not unlike miracles as we find them in the Old Testament. In Greek mythology we find a story that parallels the narrative of the deluge and the repopulation of humanity through Noah and his family. This is the story of Deucalion and Pyrrha, who created a new breed of people by throwing stones behind them. The stones that Deucalion threw turned into men, while the stones that Pyrrha threw turned into women. And while the ancient Greek epics such as the *Iliad* and the *Odyssey* mention many similar breaches of the laws of nature, perhaps the most impressive collection of miracles from the ancient world is Ovid's *Metamorphoses*, an eclectic account of transformations of humans to gods, of gods to humans, of women to men, or of humans to animals or plants.

We can find many miracles in the narratives of the New Testament, and not all are performed by Christ. There is, for instance, the resurrection of Tabitha by St. Peter, the resurrection of Eutychos by St. Paul, the various miraculous liberations of the apostles from prison, usually by angels, and even an unusual miracle of healing performed not directly by Peter, but by his shadow (Acts 5).

Generally speaking, biblical miracles as well as miracles that are mentioned in later narratives may be divided in several categories: miracles of resurrections, miracles of healing, miracles of punishment, miracles of protection, and even miracles of natural interest, such as the change of the hand of Moses into snow and back into natural flesh in the book of Exodus; the miracle of the darkness, the earthquake, and the other signs that followed the death of Jesus on the cross. Systematizing miracles may be useful if we want to understand the numerous ways God has acted in a miraculous way.

Another way to look into miracles, however, is to divide them into categories of those that were necessary for livelihood—such as the sustenance of the Israelites in the desert, the protection of the three children in the furnace, or the liberation of Paul from prison—and those whose main purpose was to demonstrate the power of God. Perhaps, ultimately, all miracles may be said to belong to the second category to some extent because they all demonstrate the power of God. Still, it is important to note that there are several miracles that do not seem to serve any other practical purpose. The healing of the blind by Christ and the relevant narrative in John's Gospel give us an insight, as it were, to the mind of Christ as he is about to heal him. The man Jesus heals was born blind, according to John 9:3, so that "the works of God should be revealed in him."

This way to approach the miracle explains something about it, which perhaps becomes more evident if we consider the biblical narrative in its liturgical context. Sometimes priests, theologians, and preachers complain that there are far too many miracle stories in the Bible and in liturgical readings, to the detriment of teachings and moral examples. Yet the church chose to include many such stories in the Gospels in the first place, and to make them regular parts of the readings in Eucharistic gatherings. What is the point of this?

It is far too simple to read the miracles of healing as isolated instances that show the compassion of Christ, but it is tempting to do so if the life of Jesus is seen as a narrative story. In this case, the simplest way to understand miracles of healing is to see them as miracles of compassion: Jesus healed the paralytic, the blind, or the lepers because he felt compassion for their misfortune. This is a problematic view because it implies some sort of unexplained tension between the world and the will of God. If Christ was compassionate enough to be moved by the sight of a leper or a paralytic and heal them, surely he would be compassionate enough to heal all paralytics and all lepers, everyone who shared in their misfortune, even those not lucky enough to be around when the Son of God was walking in the streets of Jerusalem with his disciples. This becomes even more problematic in the case of death and resurrection. If God was compassionate enough to raise Lazarus, why stop there and not stop death with a word, once and for all? This approach unavoidably leads to several theological problems.

On the other hand, we understand something very different if we remember that the Gospel readings, as a constituent part of the Eucharistic gatherings, often concentrate on events that reveal something about the kingdom of heaven. In this way the miracle of healing is not something that may be seen as an act of compassion, but as an act of revelation. It does not say much about the leper, the blind, or the paralytic, but it says something about Christ and the kingdom of heaven: it demonstrates that in the kingdom of heaven there are no lepers, blind people, or paralytics, and that Christ is the way to the kingdom. The miracle of resurrection shows this even more clearly: as death is linked directly to the fall of humanity, life in Christ, life in the kingdom of heaven, is a condition that is not subject to the effects of that fall. We can understand this more clearly and we can hear the voice of the Gospels more loudly when we consider the Gospel readings within their natural context, in the Eucharistic gathering, which is nothing less than a first taste of the kingdom of heaven. Everything that happens there reveals this eschatological dimension as much as possible.

From this perspective we can look at miracles not as instances where the laws of nature are suspended, which would be the most common definition of a miracle, but as something very different. The understanding of a miracle as a breach of the laws of nature, and as a deviation from the normal state of things, gives the impression that God, as the Aristotelian prime mover, defined the laws of the universe, created the world according to these laws, gave the first push to the well-constructed machine that is the cosmos, and stepped back, allowing it to operate on its own, without a need for further intervention. Occasionally, and for reasons that only he knows, he intervenes in the natural order of things. Either directly, or through his saints, he performs certain miraculous actions that, while they are seen as temporary suspensions of the natural laws, do not contradict the model of a God who has stepped back from his world. A miracle is an exception, which suggests that the normal state of things does not need miracles.

On the other hand, the understanding of a miracle as a foretaste or an insight into the kingdom of heaven shows something very different. According to this, God never abandoned his world, he never really stepped back. A restoration of the directness between humanity and God that existed before the fall of Adam and Eve, or perhaps even more correctly, a projection into a future time when the contact between humanity and God will be so immediate that no temple will exist in the kingdom of God, "for the Lord God Almighty and the Lamb are its temple" (Rev. 21:22), makes us think of a universe where God is explicitly present everywhere, and it is evident to everyone that he sustains all existence directly. And despite the fall of the past and the separation from God that we experience in the present age, the miracles of Christ and the saints show that the kingdom of heaven, though in the future, is also immanent, behind a curtain that is lifted by the presence of Christ.

When we understand miracles in this way, we realize that they reveal the world and the presence of God in it as it really is, as it is reflected in its eternal and true nature, and not as we perceive it through the transience and distortion of sin in the fallen world. Therefore, the miracle is much more than a teaching. The miracle reveals and demonstrates, rather than teaches and exhorts. And yet, as we also saw in the case of

the gap in the narrative of the Resurrection from the Gospels, the miracle needs our active participation. Our free response to the miracle,
whether in the form of an acceptance or a rejection, is an essential part
of the miracle itself.

This understanding of the miracle perhaps says something about the
difference between the miracles of God and magic: the event of the
miracle is an act of divine revelation and love and it includes in some
way the people who witness it, whereas a magic act (whether an act of an
illusionist or of the devil) is primarily understood as a self-contained event
that supposedly happens because of the power of *things* or the power of
the magician. Magic, with its concentration on the supposed power of
things, people, or spirits, tries to disassociate God from the world, but
at the same time, by placing faith in the power of things and not in the
power of prayer and of our connection with God, it operates in a way that
aspires to be mechanistic, which does not involve our own participation at
a deeper level. What we find with prayer, for instance, is that it opens the
possibility for our soul to move in a certain way that can meet God. More
often than not, when we pray to God we really ask him to guide us, to
teach us to do his will, and reveal to us the wisdom and the inner meaning
of the events that trouble us. We ask him to make a change inside us rather
than to change the external circumstances of our life.

The Miracle of the Transfiguration

We can discern all these aspects of the divine miracle in the
Transfiguration of Christ. The Transfiguration is the miracle that,
more than any of the other miracles that Christ performed, may be
described and understood in this somewhat more nuanced approach
to miracles. It was certainly not a miracle with a utilitarian component,
but a miracle that was performed only for the sake of divine revelation.
In other words, there was nobody who was healed, raised from the

dead, or benefited in other practical ways from the change of the appearance of Jesus.

In his Transfiguration Christ gave us the extent and the template of his miraculous power, and this helps us understand something more about the apophatic miracle of the Resurrection. Although the Resurrection of Christ is, by all accounts, the first and the most important among the miracles of Christ and all the things he did for us, the church has passed in silence many of the things that have to do with it. The Transfiguration, on the other hand, offers itself as the event on which to study the anatomy of the miracle.

There are many questions that could help us study this divine revelation. We can ask *what* was revealed, *who* was revealed, *who* received and *who* participated in the revelation, and *how* did this revelation take place.

To address the first question—what was revealed—we may take a look at the paragraphs that precede the Transfiguration narrative in the synoptic Gospels, as well as what the tradition of the church has to say. All three narratives—Mark, Matthew, and Luke—start their account of the events that led to the Transfiguration of Christ with a discussion that ends in almost exactly the same way: "There are some standing here who shall not taste death till they see the Son of Man coming in His kingdom" (Matt. 16:28), or, "There are some standing here who will not taste death till they see the kingdom of God present with power" (Mk. 9:1), or, "There are some standing here who shall not taste death till they see the kingdom of God" (Lk. 9:27).

In all three cases this mysterious prediction of Christ about "some standing here" who will see "the kingdom of God" before they die seems to be fulfilled by what follows immediately afterward. The three narratives give a direct connection between this promise and the Transfiguration, because all of them proceed immediately with the narrative of the Transfiguration, specifying that it took place six (Matthew and Mark) or eight (Luke) days after these words had been said. This suggests that what the three disciples saw on the high mountain was nothing less than a revelation of the kingdom of God.

The tradition of the church, the early Fathers and writers who wrote commentaries on the Transfiguration of Christ, gives the same conclusion. The *Apocalypse of Peter*, written in the second century, describes the Transfiguration even more directly as a revelation of the kingdom:

> And my Lord Jesus Christ our King said to me: "Let us go to the holy mountain." And his apostles went with him, praying. And behold there were two men there, and we could not look upon their faces, for a light came from them, shining more than the sun, and their raiment also was shining, and cannot be described, and nothing is sufficient to be compared to them in this world. And the sweetness of them . . . that no mouth is able to utter the beauty of their appearance, for their aspect was astonishing and wonderful. And the other, great, I say, shone in his aspect above crystal. Like the flower of roses is the appearance of the color of his aspect and of his body . . . his head. And upon his shoulders and on their foreheads was a crown of nard woven of fair flowers. As the rainbow in the water, so was their hair. And such was the comeliness of their countenance, adorned with all manner of ornament. And when we saw them on a sudden, we marveled. And I drew near to the Lord Jesus Christ and said to him: "O my Lord, who are these?" And he said to me: "They are Moses and Elijah." And I said to him: "Abraham and Isaac and Jacob and the rest of the righteous fathers?" And he showed us a great garden, open, full of fair trees and blessed fruits, and of the odor of perfumes. The fragrance thereof was pleasant and came even to us. And thereof saw I much

fruit. And my Lord and God Jesus Christ said to me: "Have you seen the companies of the fathers? As is their rest, such also is the honor and the glory of them that are persecuted for my righteousness' sake." And I rejoiced and believed and understood that which is written in the book of my Lord Jesus Christ. And I said to him: "O my Lord, will you that I make here three tabernacles, one for you, and one for Moses, and one for Elijah?" And he said to me in wrath: "Satan makes war against you, and has veiled your understanding; and the good things of this world prevail against you. Your eyes therefore must be opened and your ears unstopped that a tabernacle, not made with men's hands, which my heavenly Father has made for me and for the elect." And we beheld it and were full of gladness. And behold, suddenly there came a voice from heaven, saying: "This is my beloved Son in whom I am well pleased: my commandments." And then came a great and exceeding white cloud over our heads and bare away our Lord and Moses and Elijah. And I trembled and was afraid: and we looked up and the heaven opened and we beheld men in the flesh, and they came and greeted our Lord and Moses and Elijah and went into another heaven. And the word of the scripture was fulfilled: This is the generation that seeks him and seeks the face of the God of Jacob. And great fear and commotion was there in heaven and the angels pressed one upon another that the word of the scripture might be fulfilled which says: Open the gates, you princes. Thereafter was the heaven shut, that had been open. And we prayed and went down from the mountain, glorifying God, which has written the names of the righteous in heaven in the book of life. (ETHIOPIC APOCALYPSE OF PETER)

This text shows something important in the context of the entire ministry of Christ, and also in the context of the work of the church. The tradition of the early church sees a connection between the Transfiguration and the Passion of Christ, in that he wanted to give to his disciples a view of the kingdom of God, about which he had often talked to them, in anticipation of the difficult times that were waiting ahead. It was necessary to see the divine light of the Transfiguration at the end of the tunnel of the Crucifixion. The exhortation to the narrow gate, the asceticism and the challenges of the Christian life, the Crucifixion that we share with Christ would be useless if they could not help us find our way to the kingdom of God. But what Christ chose to do was not to give to his disciples and to humanity only words and instructions, but to lift, even if briefly, the curtain that separates this world from the presence of God, and give to his disciples the experience of the kingdom.

The church does something similar. It is true that the lives of most Christians, and even the lives of many saints, do not include the extraordinary experience of the light of God—although such experiences have certainly been attested repeatedly throughout the history of the church. But the main work of the church, from which every other task flows, is to make manifest the sacramental presence of Christ, and to give a foretaste, as much as this is possible, of the kingdom of God. This is exactly what it attempts to do and what it achieves in the Eucharistic act.

It is true that many saints of the church, and even many sinners, were given the gift of the experience of the divine light, or visions of Christ, of Mary, of angels, or of saints. But such visions are not connected in any way with the spiritual ascent of the Christian as spiritual awards. The beatific or ecstatic vision should not be seen as something that may be achieved through prayer, fast, vigilance, or any other ascetic and pious act. Such visions may be signs of sainthood, but as the Desert Fathers warn repeatedly, they may also be traps of the devil. The first danger is that the person who has them may be tempted to think of them as confirmations of holiness, self-righteousness, and self-importance. Another danger is that the experience can become a goal in itself, while the goal of the ascetic and spiritual struggle is different. For such reasons, the church and the Christian tradition were always very careful in the way they approached the visionary experience. The normal experience of the presence of God in the church is not connected with such visions. It is connected, on the other hand, with the sacramental presence of Christ, with the transformation that the Holy Spirit brings, with the Divine Liturgy, which is nothing less than a reflection and a projection of the kingdom of God into the here and now, and with the liturgical experience of the transfiguration of the entire church in Christ.

Stepping into the Kingdom of God

The entire Eucharist, the Divine Liturgy as it is known in the East, is a stepping into the kingdom of God, albeit in a partial way, in a symbolic or liturgical way. Unlike other services of the church, which start with a different prayer, the opening line of the Divine Liturgy tells us where we are: "Blessed is the Kingdom of the Father and of the Son, and of the Holy Spirit." Similarly, many of the words and prayers of the Divine Liturgy place us after, and not before, the Second Coming of Christ—as in the prayer of the commemoration of what Christ has done for us and for our salvation. The priest says a prayer at the middle of the service that recounts what Christ has done for us: "The Cross, the Tomb, the Resurrection on the third day, the Ascension into heaven, the Sitting at the right hand, the Second and glorious Coming again." We *remember* the Second Coming in the Eucharistic service, as if it has already happened, and as if we are already in the New Jerusalem.

But such textual examples are simply indicative of the fact that the entire liturgical life of the Orthodox world revolves precisely around "making present" the kingdom of heaven in the here and now, through the sacramental body and blood of Christ. This is the primary, if not the only, work that defines the church, the only thing that it is necessary for the church to do, and the only thing that the church can do. Everything else, every other good thing that comes from the church, every act of charity, every act of support, every sermon, and every prayer, is a result of these two things. Humanitarian aid, care for the sick and the orphans, social justice, and other good works that are often associated with Christianity express an active concern for the quality of life of our fellow human beings, on the one hand, but are the work of the church as much as they are the work of the state, of nongovernmental organizations and other similar structures. Such work of servitude does indeed exemplify some Christian values, but this work is not what defines the Christian church.

A very important level of revelation that we see in the Transfiguration is the direct revelation of Christ's divinity to Peter, John, and James. In some ways this is the primary description of the event of the Transfiguration, or even its shortest definition. However, when we look a little closer into the way this revelation took place, we realize that it is much more subtle and complex than an overt manifestation of a fact.

A problem, for instance, that was discussed by the Fathers of the church is where and how, exactly, the change happened. Did Christ change? Did his nature change? Did he become something that he was not before the ascent to Mount Thabor? The biblical text uses expressions that touch on the change of his appearance, but they do not proceed much deeper than that. We come across a problem if we presume that the nature of Christ changed during his Transfiguration. Such a presumption would imply a change in the nature of God, which is, by any understanding of God, impossible. Could we then say that it was a change of his humanity? Could we say, as some early Christian writers did, that the human nature of Christ was pushed aside for a moment, so that the three disciples could see his divinity? That may not sound as difficult, but it is possible to see this "stepping aside" of the humanity of Christ as a compromise of his Incarnation, as if the transfigured state of Christ revealed something about what Christ is that could not be seen in his incarnated state.

It may be possible to argue the latter point to a limited extent, because there was indeed a change. The change in the appearance of the body and face of Christ was seen by the early church as a revelation of his divinity. This revelation, however, can allow us to appreciate the Transfiguration not as a negation of the Incarnation, but as its fulfillment. The Incarnation of Christ was the union of the divine and the human nature in one person without a compromise of the two natures, without any confusion between them, and in such a way the two could not be divided or separated. But though it was possible to look at Christ and see him as a human, the Transfiguration shows that Christ's divinity, which was normally hidden, was also fully present. Nevertheless, although there is some value in saying that the humanity of Christ stepped aside during his Transfiguration so that his divinity could be seen more clearly, there must be a more complete interpretation of the change that happened on Mount Thabor that would pay respect to the participation of both sides of Christ's nature—human and divine. In order to understand such an interpretation, we have to start from the position that the divinity of Christ is something that needed to be constantly discovered.

There is a lot to be said about the hiddenness of the divinity of Christ. Even if we suppose that some people in his time had realized completely who he was, we just cannot imagine this kind of dialogue between two people who lived in Nazareth and knew Jesus when he was a child:

"I hear noise in the street. Can you see what is going on?"

"Oh, nothing to worry about. It is the Son of God, playing with his friends!" Even his closest disciples were at a constant journey of discovery with him. In the synoptic Gospels they were trying to understand at every step of the way something more about who their teacher really was. John's Gospel is written from a different point of view and for a different reason, and it starts with the affirmation of the divinity of Christ as the Logos. In the Gospels of Mark, Matthew, and Luke, on the other hand, we can follow the constant perplexity of the disciples as they only gradually realize who Christ is—and they do so fully only after his Resurrection. This process of engagement with the mystery that is Christ is part of the recognition that leads to his divinity, equally true for the disciples of Christ as it is for us today.

And here we find the second part of his manifestation in divine form: since we cannot expect that there was any change in Christ himself during the event of the Transfiguration, any change that took place actually occurred in the disciples and not in Christ. Through the act of the Holy Spirit and the grace of God, it was possible for them to start seeing their master in a different way. What happened to them was not that they understood intellectually how Jesus was the fulfillment of the prophecies, the Savior, the very God. Instead, the Holy Spirit gave them the chance to enter into an ontological relationship with Christ, allowing themselves to be united with him as much as it was possible for them, and through this union to understand something of him.

The third part of the revelation of the Godhead in the Transfiguration of Christ is the revelation of the Father through the Son. As in the case of his Baptism, Christ's filial relationship with the Father is revealed by the words of the Father himself, which were almost identical to the words that were heard in the Jordan River at the Baptism of Christ. But this time more is revealed. The humanity of Christ and his Incarnation were proclaimed by the archangel Gabriel to Mary and were manifested at his birth, but on Mount Thabor Christ's divinity is also somehow made visible in front of witnesses. The inapproachable Father reveals his divinity through his Son and in this way imparts any part of the Godhead that can actually be seen, even if it results in an extraordinarily intense brightness that the eyes of Peter, John, and James cannot fully process and see.

The presence of Moses and Elijah demonstrates Christ's divinity very clearly. Of all the righteous figures of the past, of all the prophets of the Hebrew tradition, these two were singled out and brought to the mountain of the Transfiguration. Why these two and only these two? It is perhaps not hard to see the prominence of Moses, the man who essentially founded the Jewish nation and the Jewish state, but one could say that the honor of the second person of the Old Testament to be brought back from the dead might fall on Abraham, David, or Solomon—or maybe on all of them. Why these two?

Moses and Elijah have something in common. According to Scripture, both of them requested to see God and had that request denied. It is true that the Old Testament is not very clear about things that have to do with the vision of God. The dialogue between God and Moses in Exodus 33:18–23 is fairly well known. In this passage Moses asks God to allow him to see him in his glory, to which God replies, "no man shall see me, and live." What we read here sounds unequivocal, although several other passages in the Old Testament, even passages in the book of Exodus, give a different kind of testimony that implies it is perfectly possible to see God. For instance, there are the seventy elders who saw, ate, and drank with God (Exod. 24:9–11), or Hagar, who marvels at being alive after she has seen God (Gen. 16:7–16), or Jacob, who exclaims, "I have seen God face to face" (Gen. 32:30).

Nevertheless, the reluctance of God to reveal himself completely "in his glory" to Moses and to Elijah suggests that these two did not just ask to receive some sort of visual sign given to them by God, but a complete visual revelation of the Godhead, something that was not possible at that time. Yet their presence on the mountain of the Transfiguration may be understood precisely as the fulfillment of their desire to see God. They had asked to see the God of the Old Testament, and yet it is Christ they came to see face to face. Far from a confusion between the person of the Father and the person of the

Son in the manner that the early church condemned along with its proponent Sabellius (the priest who promoted the view that the same entity could be seen through the "masks" of the Father in the Old Testament, the Son in the New Testament, and the Holy Spirit in the church), the fulfillment of the vision of Moses and Elijah during the Transfiguration was that they were allowed to see the divine light of the Father shine through the Son. Although they were faced with the second person of the Trinity, they could finally see the same divinity that they had desired and requested to see when they addressed the first person of the Trinity.

Revelations of Salvation

Although the Transfiguration is primarily an event associated with Christ, we can see that the entire Trinity was revealed in it. The Transfiguration was a Trinitarian revelation that was given dynamically, through certain levels of participation, to the ones who witnessed it. We can discern these levels if we consider the Transfiguration scene as it appears in Eastern iconography. Christ, flanked by Moses and Elijah, who are sometimes included in the luminous aureole that symbolizes the light that emanates from him, corresponds to the kingdom of heaven. There, the dead are no longer dead but are serene participants of the divinity of Christ. Moses and Elijah converse with Christ, thus indicating that the kingdom of God is understood in terms of a continuous communion between Christ and the saints. More than that, the Fathers of the church talk about a different degree of communion between Christ and the two righteous prophets, as opposed to the three fallen and terrified apostles. We can see what this means very clearly in a schematic way in the iconography of the Transfiguration according to the Orthodox tradition.

The most prominent characteristic of the icon of the Transfiguration is the light that emanates from Christ and extends to the Old Testament prophets, as well as to Peter, John, and James. As is the case with most icons, this light is independent of any sources of natural light, such as the sun or the moon. Instead, it is the kind of light that, as in John's Gospel, appears to be synonymous with divinity. Not everyone is participating in it to the same degree. Moses and Elijah, the righteous and perfected ones who dare talk with the Transfigured Christ face to face, are embraced and often are enveloped by the light that emanates from Christ. On the other hand, the rays that emanate from the body of Christ reach all the way to the fallen apostles, but their impact does not seem to be nearly as dramatic as the impact of the light on Moses and Elijah. Not accidentally, their bodies are always portrayed in a much more troubled and contorted way compared with the serene presence of Moses and Elijah, and the hieratic, solemn presence of Christ. And yet, all five of them are turned toward Christ, and they participate to different extents in the light that emanates from him.

What we see if we consider the icon of the Transfiguration in this way is an image of the church. Christ, in the middle, seems almost to be made of light. But this is the key to understand the whole event through the icon: the body of Christ *is* light, and it extends beyond the physical boundaries of his human body. In slightly more theological terms, what defines Christ is the union of the created and the uncreated, the human and the divine, the visible and the invisible. This union extends to Moses, Elijah, Peter, John, and James, as we saw, but they become body of Christ in a different way. The union of the created and the uncreated may be seen also in them, but they must receive the light of union from Christ, who as a divine lens sends the light of the Father to them. Through Christ's outpouring of his divinity as portrayed in the icon of the Transfiguration, he Christ-ifies those who step into his light and become part of his extended body. This is also the way such Christification takes place in the church.

This somewhat simplistic outline shows, even schematically, how the Transfiguration of Christ reveals so much about salvation. The resplendent body of Christ makes sense only within a Trinitarian context, with the Holy Spirit making it possible for the ones who are led by Christ to start seeing him as the radiance of the Father. This is the revelation of Christ as he really is, seen by the eyesight that has been touched by the Holy Spirit. But although there is a long tradition of ascetics who were granted the miracle of seeing the Uncreated Light of the Godhead, the light that emanates from the body of Christ and makes his divinity present even to the most remote or the most insignificant parts of the Creation, is not an affair of the individual. The entire event of the Transfiguration consists of a setting apart, but also of an ecclesial communion between heaven and earth, which is formed with Christ as its focal point. Light as life, light as the grace of God, light as the presence of Christ is given not as a reward for the difficult task of ascending the Thabor of moral perfection, but as a gift that God offers freely and that we have to receive as participants in his glory and his divinity.

The Transfiguration, approached as a miracle, shows all this. If, as demonstrated earlier, a miracle is a way to experience and accept the offering that is given freely by God to us, the Transfiguration must be recognized as the greatest miracle of divine revelation. In the light of the Transfigured Christ, we can see the kingdom of heaven, the Trinitarian life of God, the mystery of the church, and the mystery of our own salvation. We can see our invitation to a union with the mystical body of Christ, a union with his own divinity, with the source, the truth, and the mystical principle of all life.

5
LORD, IT IS GOOD FOR US TO BE HERE
The Experience of the Uncreated Light

I N ADDITION TO ALL THE OTHER PERSPECTIVES that we have explored, the narrative of the Transfiguration is impressive as the description of an experience. The dazzling light that radiated from the face and the entire body of Jesus, and also the feeling of well-being that his disciples felt, make it a powerful experience that changed the lives of those who witnessed it. Yet, although it was exceptional, it was not unique. In fact, a long tradition of experiences of the same metaphysical light that shone on Peter, John, and James on Thabor can be traced in the Eastern Christian world, even to our own time.

Orthodox Christianity identifies this metaphysical light as the presence, manifestation, and operation of God, recognizing it to be a light of the same kind as the light of the Transfiguration. In fact, we often refer to it as the "Thaboric Light."

The literature of the Thaboric Light is well established and respected in the East, and includes biblical examples such as St. Paul and St. Stephen, countless desert ascetics, patristic figures such as St. Symeon the New Theologian, but also people who lived in modern times, such as the Greek monks Paisios and Porphyrios, who died only a few years ago. Until fairly recently, the Western world was somewhat apprehensive about the truthfulness of these accounts. The publication of the works of Gregory Palamas and Symeon the New Theologian within the last few years offered a way to approach this kind of experience. Even so, there are several ecstatic accounts of similar nature in the Western tradition, with similar experiences of a metaphysical and wondrous light, such as in the Celtic legends of St. Columba. There are countless similar accounts of experiences of the divine light in ancient, medieval, and modern sources, but let us look at two of the most celebrated examples, the first from the tenth century, written by St. Symeon the New Theologian who, like St. Paul, writes in the third person when he describes his own experience:

> One day, as [Symeon] stood and recited "God, have mercy upon me, a sinner," uttering it with his mind rather than his mouth, suddenly a flood of divine radiance appeared from above and filled the entire room. As this happened the young man lost all awareness of his surroundings and forgot that he was in a house or that he was under a roof. He saw nothing but light all around him and did not know if he was standing on the ground. He was not afraid of falling; he was not concerned with the world, nor did anything pertaining to men and corporeal beings enter into his mind. Instead, he was wholly in the presence of immaterial light and seemed to himself to have turned into light. Oblivious of the entire world he was filled with tears and with ineffable joy and gladness. His mind then ascended to heaven and beheld yet another light, which was clearer than that which was close at hand.[16]

The second example is from the nineteenth century, a transcript of a conversation between St. Seraphim of Sarov and his spiritual child, Nicholas Motovilov:

> "The grace of the Holy Spirit is the light which lightens man. And indeed, the Lord has often demonstrated before

many witnesses how the grace of the Holy Spirit operates with regard to those people whom He has sanctified and illumined by His great visitation. Remember Moses after his conversation with God on Mount Sinai. He shone with such an extraordinary light that people could not look at him, and he had to cover his face. Remember the Transfiguration of the Lord on Mount Thabor. A great light surrounded Him and 'His garments became shining, exceedingly white like snow' and His apostles fell on their faces from fear. In the same way the grace of the Holy Spirit of God manifests itself in an ineffable light to all to whom God reveals its activity."

"But how," I asked Father Seraphim, "can I know that I am in the grace of the Holy Spirit? I need to understand completely."

Father Seraphim then took me very firmly by the shoulders and said, "We are both, you and I, in the Spirit of God this moment, my son. Why do you not look at me?"

"I cannot look, Father," I replied, "because great flashes of lightning are springing from your eyes. Your face shines with more light than the sun and my eyes ache from the pain."

"Don't be frightened, friend of God," Father Seraphim said. "You yourself have now become as bright as I am. You are now yourself in the fullness of the Spirit of God: otherwise you would not be able to see me like this. Why don't you look at me, my son? Just look, don't be afraid! The Lord is with us!"

At these words, I looked at his face and was seized with an even greater sense of trembling awe. Imagine in the center of the sun, in the most dazzling brilliance of his noontime rays, the face of a man talking to you. You see the movement of his lips, the changing expression of his eyes, you hear his voice, you feel that someone is holding his hands on your shoulders. Yet you do not see his hands or his body, but only a blinding light spreading around for several yards, illuminating with its brilliant sheen both the bank of snow covering the glade and the snowflakes that fall on me and the great Starets. Can you imagine the state I was in?

"How do you feel now?" Father Seraphim asked me.

"Extraordinarily well!" I said.

"How 'well'? How exactly do you feel?"

"I feel," I replied, "such quiet and peace in my soul that I have no words to express them."

"And what else do you feel?" Father Seraphim asked me.

"An extraordinary sweetness."

"And what else do you feel?"

"An extraordinary joy in all my heart."

"What else do you feel, friend of God?"

"An extraordinary warmth," I replied.

"This warmth, then, is not in the air but comes from within us. It is that very warmth of which the Holy Spirit makes us cry out to the Lord in prayer: 'Warm me with the warmth of Thy Holy Spirit.' And this is how it should be in fact, because the grace of God ought to dwell within us, in our hearts, for the Lord said: 'The Kingdom of God is within you.' By the Kingdom of God the Lord meant the grace of the Holy Spirit. The Kingdom of God is now within you, and the grace of the Holy Spirit shines upon us and warms us from without as well, and, filling the air around us with many varied fragrances, it sweetens our senses with heavenly sweetness and floods our hearts with unutterable joy."[17]

The spiritual literature of the Christian East is filled with similar examples. It is always prudent to consider these in the light of theology and church life.

Since the Enlightenment, we live in a culture that considers itself grounded in rational principles. Also, we know that there are far too many self-proclaimed mystics, too many seers and prophets who believe they have powers that allow them to penetrate time and space and see beyond them. While it is possible to believe in the ecstatic experience, it is also possible to believe in medical and psychological conditions that may produce similar results, and yet have nothing to do with spirituality at any level.

The ecstatic experience in itself has no meaning. Starting from the actions of Jesus Christ as they are described in the Gospels, the miraculous healings, the transformation of water to wine, the raising of the dead, and all the other miracles he performed were not simply demonstrations of power. The point was not so much to show that Christ could do things that mortals could not and therefore to convince his followers that he was different from them. Instead, the miracles revealed something about the way God exists: not bound by time, space, or necessity, but in complete freedom.

But what appears as blanket scepticism here is also not an attempt to dismiss all possibilities of extraordinary experiences. Any real extraordinary experience by itself is not necessarily something good or holy. This is something that the early monastics—people who fled their cities and their villages and chose a life of prayer in the Egyptian and the Palestinian desert in the third and the fourth century—knew very well. Sometimes a young or inexperienced monk would have a vision, but more experienced monks advised him to disregard most of these visions, or at least to consider seriously that they might not be sent by God, but by Satan instead. These monks considered themselves at constant battle with the powers of darkness; they understood that the devil can use human weaknesses to prevail upon them. And the most dangerous, in a long list of weaknesses or vices, is pride. There is nothing more dangerous for someone who is eager to advance in the spiritual life and the ascetic struggle than a vision or experience that may seem to be an affirmation of his or her sanctity. Pride threatens even experienced ascetics. The ascetic tradition advises much careful discernment before a vision is accepted as something actually sent from God.

There is a dramatic account from the lives of the ascetics of the desert, where a monk had a vision of Christ. Christ, in the vision, told him that he could stop his struggle, that he had attained perfection and he had become a saint. The monk thought that this was a very strange thing for Christ to say and he asked him to prove that he was indeed Christ by showing him the signs of humility, the signs of the nails on his hands and his feet. Hearing this, the demonic vision—for only a vision of demonic temptation could suggest that there is an end in the ascent toward God—disappeared in smoke. According to the story, the monk was saved because instead of looking for signs of achievement and pride in his own life, he looked for signs of humility.

So ultimately, we are faced with a body of tradition of divine encounters, visions sent from God, and ecstatic experiences, but also with a boundless sea of false visionaries, hallucinations, and visions that may be genuine, but are not sent from God. As Christ says in Matthew 7:15–20, we recognize false prophets by the fruit they bear: "a good tree cannot bear bad fruit, nor can a bad tree bear good fruit." In the case of visions and visionaries, the question is what happens to them or to their followers after the ecstatic vision. Are they brought closer to salvation? Are they brought closer to God? Or are they distracted from the Creator, admiring the creature?

The light of the Transfiguration puts this question into perspective. Several centuries ago, Barlaam, a monk from southern Italy who visited the renowned monastic community of Mount Athos in the north of

Greece, was struck by the accounts of several monks who apparently did not do much more than withdraw to increasingly deeper levels of prayer using a very simple prayer formula—only one phrase, which they kept repeating for hours. What scandalized Barlaam was not so much that these monks retreated into the stillness of their minds, but that they claimed to see God in some of their most deep prayer sessions—or rather, they saw an exceptionally bright light and took it as a vision of God. Moreover, many other monks, theologians, and bishops of the church seemed to take them seriously. Barlaam became quite concerned.

He tried to learn something more about the prayer practices of these monks, but apparently what he was given was the kind of practical advice elder monks give to younger ones who are trained in the ways of long prayer sessions. In short, there was not enough theological or philosophical basis in what Barlaam saw there. In addition, this looked like heresies that Christianity had seen before, which viewed salvation as something reserved for those who could denounce the world and ascend to higher levels of consciousness by their incessant prayer. Therefore, Barlaam questioned publically these practices.

Since *ecstatic* literally means "outside the body," this lowly view of corporeal existence does not take seriously the view that all matter was created by God, and the human body—the same lowly body that was united with God through the Incarnation of Christ—was fashioned directly by him. This view of salvation by prayer and the wish for an individual ecstatic ascent to the divine realm contradicts, or rather insults, as it were, the ministry and the work of Christ. The Incarnation, Crucifixion, and Resurrection of Christ were acts that were worked out for the salvation of the world—*necessary* acts for the salvation of the world. These acts address the state of humanity and its reconciliation with God. Since Christ is the only connection between the created and the uncreated world, it is simply not possible to talk about an ascent to God without the participation of Christ.

Experiencing the Holy Spirit

The true ecstatic and ascetic experience is connected with the operation of the Holy Spirit as the person of the Trinity who makes the kingdom of God present. Scripture reminds us that "the wind [Spirit] blows where it wishes" (Jn. 3:8), and has spoken through the prophets of old, but it may also be found in prophetic and genuinely charismatic expressions of faith in the present. Visionary experience is connected to the operation of the Holy Spirit, as was the experience of Peter, John, and James in front of the Transfigured Jesus. The Holy Spirit dispenses grace, grants illuminations, guides, visits, and inspires, yet its work in the economy of salvation is very specific: to bring people together in the name of Christ, to form the body of Christ out of those who respond to the call of God (as we see with the manifestation of the Holy Spirit at Pentecost, when people from different traditions were brought together and formed a community in the name of Christ), and to introduce them here and now to the kingdom of heaven, which will be revealed fully at the end of time.

The plan of salvation involves the full and specific participation of every person of the Trinity. For Christian theology there is nothing that Christ does in which he does not refer to the Father and also involve the Holy Spirit in some way. Naturally, it is possible to say the same thing in the opposite way: all the gifts, inspirations, miracles, and other operations of the Holy Spirit are, in some way, given from the Father. We say this not only because we see it in the way Jesus talks about his heavenly Father, but also because the personhood of the Father expresses all the qualities of God that are beyond any understanding and any limit—and therefore we understand the Father as the source of all divinity.

In turn, everything the Holy Spirit does serves only one purpose: to reveal Christ. We see this in the Bible, in the tradition of the church, and in the lives of the saints. The Holy Spirit inspired the Prophets of the Old Testament, but was more openly revealed in the Baptism and the Transfiguration of Christ and, foremost, at Pentecost. While the revelation of Christ in the Old Testament was prophetic and unclear, the Holy Spirit allowed the Galilean fishermen to recognize the Son of the Father in the face of their teacher. At Pentecost, on the other hand, the Holy Spirit revealed that the church and Christ were one. The life of the church from this perspective is a continuous reliving of Pentecost, where we come as individuals, but through the power of the Holy Spirit we are changed into the sacramental body of Christ.

The Holy Spirit operates in such a way that the visions, the miracles, the ecstatic experiences it grants reveal Christ and lead us to him. Sometimes, as in the case of St. Paul, the visionary experience is given as a great light or as a foretaste of the kingdom of heaven. In Scripture, as well as in the life of the church, we can see that the Holy Spirit may act on the most unexpected person, such as St. Paul while he was persecuting Christianity, or on ascetics who have lived their entire life in devoted prayer. It is not possible to say whether the Holy Spirit will visit the saint or the sinner. We know, however, that its visitation invites the receiver to a lifelong journey toward Christ. The end of this journey is the conversion and incorporation into the body of Christ.

Salvation Is Not an Escape

The Transfiguration was often understood by the saints of the church as the archetypal ecstatic experience of the divine light. It shows that the Holy Spirit does not prompt a denial of the world—and even the ascetics who left their homes and went to the desert did so in order to serve the world in a different way. Peter, in all three Gospel narratives of the Transfiguration, is overwhelmed by the vision and asks Jesus if they should erect three tents and stay on Mount Thabor. Mark's and Luke's Gospels add a comment after this question, which may be translated as, "for he did not know what to say," or, "he did not know what he was saying." Peter's question does not receive an answer from Christ in the Gospel text, and is just ignored. However, early Christian writers who comment on this biblical passage give an interesting explanation for the dismissive attitude of Christ. They write that Peter, John, and James were so overwhelmed by the ecstatic vision, which in their eyes was nothing less than the opening of Paradise, that they wanted to stay in this blissful condition permanently. This is an understandable temptation, but the ecstatic vision of the divine light is not given for its own sake. The goal is not simply to see an impressive light and to acquire an intoxicating feeling of well-being. The answer of Jesus to Peter, as it was implied in the Gospel narratives, was that this is not the end of the struggle at all. After the brilliance of the Transfiguration, Jesus has to return to the world and offer himself to the Passion and Crucifixion. Those who follow him will have to do the same and sacrifice themselves for his name. The visionary experience of light points to the difficult path that leads to the Cross.

God's work of salvation was based on the acceptance of Christ to come down to earth and to embrace the human condition in its entirety, including death. This act of condescension and sacrifice reveals, at least partly, that the nature of God is love. We often say that God is not bound by passions, because we recognize that he is not limited by necessity. However, we also recognize that in his boundless freedom he has one strong passion, which is stressed repeatedly in liturgical hymnography: his love for humanity—which made St. Basil describe God as "the manic lover of humankind."

God is the Lover and the Beloved. By responding to his love we share in his passion for humankind. Similarly, to become "like God" or to be deified, as the Eastern Christian tradition puts it, refers primarily, if not exclusively, to the journey of love that begins with the birth of God inside us, and ends with a simultaneous Passion and Resurrection. Sharing God's love means that it is impossible to love God, to desire to be with God, and to unite with him, and also not love humankind as he does. In the context of the Transfiguration, the brilliance of Christ comes with a responsibility of love. By revealing his divinity to humanity and by becoming transparent for his disciples, Jesus allowed them to see what he desired to do next, and what he invited them to: the return to the fallen world and the sacrifice.

The Transfiguration, therefore, reveals something important about salvation: salvation is not a state of perpetual bliss, a garden of pleasure— even if we make sure to describe it as "spiritual pleasure," whatever this may possibly mean—but an active participation in the presence, the being, and the work of Christ. Salvation means that the ecstatic experience, if and when it happens, is no more than a step toward the ultimate goal of the salvation of the entire world. In this context, a wish for individual salvation does not make sense. Saints understand this. Monasticism understands this, even if at a first glance we see the monk as a solitary ascetic who flees the city to save his own soul. Yet the black habit of monastics is a symbol of mourning for the fallen state of the entire world. A monk mourns not only for his own sinfulness, but also for the smallest sign that reminds him that this world has fallen from the grace of God. A monk mourns for a great disaster, for a catastrophic tsunami or for a war, but also for a bird that dies in the middle of the winter. The point is that although we ask for forgiveness personally, and we try to take responsibility for our own sins, if we think as God does and if we share in God's love for the world, we will mourn for those who have excluded themselves from salvation. We cannot remain blissfully ignorant on the top of Mount Thabor, bathed in the divine light and wishing we could stay there, while the rest of the world needs Christ. Something is incomplete. Although the foretaste of the kingdom of heaven was given on the top of Thabor, the actual way passes through the Cross.

In the Transfiguration, Christ is shown to be the connection between humanity and the kingdom of God where the blessed righteous are. The Transfiguration gives us a model of the entire drama of the connection between heaven and earth, which in all possible ways points to Christ. In the miracle of Thabor Christ presents himself as the only connection between the unapproachable divinity of the Father and the world. Christianity does not acknowledge any other way that we can see or know God. The Father, the inexpressible eternal source of divinity, may be fully known only by someone who shares his nature, who exists in the same divinity. On the other hand, the human nature of Christ has made it possible for him to be known by us, to enter human history, and to offer a way for us to address God face to face. In addition, the Incarnation and the transformative power of the Holy Spirit after Pentecost allowed us to participate in the mystical body of Christ. By becoming part of Christ, we address the Father as only his Son does.

This is the unique role of Christ, who has offered himself as the place where the meeting of God and humanity takes place. There can be no other complete connection between heaven and earth because there is nobody else who possesses and can unite both the human and the divine nature. What can we say, then, about transcendental or ecstatic experiences that may reveal something about the spiritual world, if they are not connected with Christ? Any spiritual revelation that is not connected with him—if there can be such a thing—may, at best, reveal something about the invisible world, the world of angels and demons, or even something about God, but it cannot reveal God fully and ultimately lead us to him.

The Transfiguration reveals the way salvation comes to the world through Christ. This event is at the heart of his ministry—Mark places it at the exact middle of his Gospel—because it illuminates all of the important events in the life of Christ. For this reason it reflects the connection between heaven and earth in a way that is consistent with what the life and ministry of Christ show to us. As a self-revelation that speaks to both Christ's divine and human nature, the Transfiguration is a manifestation of the Incarnation of God. As a revelation of his glory, it says something about his power over death and his Resurrection. As a reflection of his deliberate choice to come down from Mount Thabor and into the world, it anticipates his Passion. Finally, as a revelation of the inner life of the Trinity, it shows how the entire Godhead converges on the person of Christ for the salvation of humanity.

In other words, participation in Christ is not simply a participation in his blissful radiance, but a participation in all the stages that are connected with it. In order to shine with Christ, we need to experience his birth in our flesh, his baptism in the Jordan, his Passion and his Resurrection, and recognize what all of them mean in our life. The Transfiguration is not so much a separate chapter of our spiritual life, but an event that illuminates and reveals the significance of all the other Christological events in our own life.

The Presence of the Holy Spirit in the Transfiguration

The Holy Spirit has a distinct role in salvation, but precisely defining that role is a question that has perplexed and divided theologians for many centuries. The Scriptural passages that have mostly been used to understand and illustrate the power and operation of the Holy Spirit are the ones that describe Pentecost and the Baptism of Christ. In addition to them, the Transfiguration as a complete manifestation of the Trinity in the Bible also reveals a lot about the Holy Spirit, its participation in salvation, and its relationship to the other two persons of the Trinity.

The presence of the Holy Spirit in the Transfiguration is not explicitly stated in the biblical text. This should not surprise us. Early Christianity had only an elementary understanding of Trinitarian theology at the theoretical level, even if it is possible to find very strong expressions of faith in the Trinity in early Christian literature. The presence of the Holy Spirit is given in a language that flows out of the Old Testament descriptions of the Spirit of God and the cloud that guided the Israelites. Nevertheless, there is much more in the scene that shows the presence and the operation of the Holy Spirit—we could say that the entire event takes place within the Holy Spirit, which enveloped the participants as a white luminous cloud.

The Fathers of the church tried to understand what, exactly, changed during the Transfiguration, and what made Christ appear in a different form. They realized that we cannot look for this change in the nature of Christ; we must look elsewhere. If we argue that in the Transfiguration we can see the complete revelation of Christ as God and as man, then we realize that his divinity, which was fully present when he was born in Bethlehem as a helpless baby, was meant to be discovered rather than to be demonstrated plainly. In other words, the discovery of the divinity of Christ is a continuous hermeneutic process. This continuous discovery is achieved in collaboration with the Holy Spirit. The same thing is shown in the other biblical example where Christ appeared "in another form" to two of his disciples after his Resurrection, in Mark 16:12. There, too, the identity of the mysterious stranger who accompanied the two disciples eluded them until the breaking of the bread, the liturgical hermeneutic discovery of God.

Although in his Second Coming Christ will come in glory, in a full manifestation of his divinity, in his First Coming he "made himself of no reputation, taking the form of a bondservant, and coming in the likeness of men" (Phil. 2:7). Although we can follow the discovery of Christ's divinity in the synoptic Gospels, which perhaps culminates in the words of the centurion after the death of Christ, "Truly this was the Son of God!" (Matt. 27:54; Mk. 15:39), the demonstration of his divinity in the Transfiguration is clear and unequivocal. It is not a public declaration. Very few witness it—only three of the twelve disciples, and these only after they experienced the ascetic ascent to the high mountain.

The Holy Spirit offered Peter, John, and James the grace to see what they would not be able to see otherwise, and in this way changed how they were able to see. But this was not the only time the Holy Spirit has operated in this way. The tradition of the church has described this change in the people who are given this grace, as a different level of perception that they acquire, a different way of seeing and hearing. It is described as the awakening of the spiritual senses—another way to describe the continuous hermeneutic discovery of God through the Holy Spirit. Saints who were given this gift did not usually talk about it very much or very openly. Certainly, one of the things that accompany this kind of power is an extreme sense of humility, which is based in the strong understanding of the person who has had the vision that this was not something that was achieved by his own power. The touch of the grace of God is not something that can make one proud, but is something that results in the even greater gift of humility. More than that, this is an ascent into things that cannot be expressed in words and cannot be compared against the experience of everyday life. The only thing we have is pointers that show the way.

It is both interesting and impossible to try to understand the ways of the Holy Spirit. There is very little we can actually grasp, and much of this is difficult to describe because it refers to a realm very different from the world as we usually know it. Nevertheless, we can turn to experiences of saints and what has been revealed in Scripture and the tradition of the church.

The Holy Spirit always works with the cooperation of those it visits, much like Mary accepted freely to become the Mother of God. But if a person clears the obstacles that separate them from God and becomes a permanent home to the Holy Spirit, their entire being becomes imbued with the divine presence. As the saint gives himself to the Holy Spirit, some of the properties of the indwelling divinity then pass to him. Like another Mary, the saint becomes a Christ-bearer. The references of St. Paul to a life that is no more his own, but the life of Christ who lives inside him (Gal. 2), and the transformation of the individual Christians into the body of Christ that is the church (Rom. 12) witness this kind of transfiguration.

The Transfiguration of Christ offers a model that helps us understand how the grace of God works. The light that shines from Christ and opens the kingdom of heaven to Peter, John, and James changed the way their bodies worked. They began to see things "by grace," no less real and certainly not in an abstract or symbolic manner. They began to hear things that men do not normally hear, just like Paul did after his encounter with the divine light, when he was snatched to the third heaven and heard "inexpressible words, which it is not lawful for a man to utter" (2 Cor. 12:4). In the Transfiguration narrative we see the same restriction as to what was heard: the two most respected and loved prophets in the Jewish tradition appeared on Mount Thabor and started talking with Christ, yet none of the witnesses of this extraordinary scene noted what they said, other than a brief reference to the Passion and Resurrection of Jesus in Luke's Gospel. The evangelists pass that conversation in silence. Clearly, it was not very different from the "inexpressible words" that Paul heard. After all, both experiences took place in the third heaven, the kingdom of God.

After Barlaam of Calabria questioned the ecstatic experiences of the Athonite monks in the fourteenth century, one of these Athonite monks who had a deeper and more systematic understanding of the experiences and theology of the church wrote a number of detailed expositions of the spirituality of the ceaseless prayer and the experience of the light. This monk, St. Gregory Palamas, is still recognized as one of the greatest theologians of the Greek Church. One of the challenges he faced was to situate the contemplative tradition and the ecstatic experience of the light of the Transfiguration within the work of the church. In other words, it became necessary to compare and contrast the solitary experience of the light with the sacrament of communion.

We often think of sacramental communion as a "thing" that has received a blessing from above and been transformed into something our senses cannot understand. While there is some value in referring to the Eucharist as the focus and center of the sacramental change of the people of God into his image, the presence of Christ and the transformation of the people of God exceed this approach. Gregory Palamas and his disciples could see something of the ecstatic experience in the Eucharistic communion—not in the sense of the extraordinary visionary experience, but in the dynamic dimension of the sacrament, during which the same outpouring of God's love is taking place, even if it is not evident. The solitary experience of the light of God reveals a small part of the magnitude of God's presence, but it does not show anything that is not also true for the Eucharist. The Holy Spirit invites everyone to the ascent beyond the words, and Christ may be born inside anyone who responds to the call. While the experiences of the Athonite monks that Gregory Palamas defended were exceptional, they were revealing and pointing toward the liturgical recognition of God in the person of the other, in the community that is gathered in the name of Jesus Christ. The kingdom of God in the Bible is usually depicted as a great feast and as a communion of saints. Without this end, the solitary experience of light does not take root.

Transfiguration in the Church

There is no better way to describe the Eucharistic offering than to talk about it as the offering of free and unconditional salvation, and as the transfiguration of the human condition. However, there are far too many churches, congregations, and parishes in the Christian world that struggle to provide it because they struggle to maintain their sense of the Transfiguration.

We can visit a Sunday service in a Christian church and notice what is happening there. We will not be able to understand the services if we try to assume a critical gaze that does not leave space for faith.

We cannot approach the services only with a scientific eye, as an anthropologist might observe patterns of social interaction in a newly discovered culture. Some faith is necessary just to get started and to enter the hermeneutics of the mystery. On the other hand, the liturgical service is supposed to cultivate this faith, to draw us in, and to give us an understanding of heaven and salvation that no words and arguments can convey. This liturgical mystery, this distance between the words that say little and the practice that says much more, is one of the founding and constituting elements of Christianity. For this reason Christianity needs to expect a lot from its liturgical services.

But this is not always the impression we get when we visit a church. Mechanical chanting and saying of the services imply that the power and the revelation are in the words themselves and no further. A pitfall on the other side is to resort to a strongly emotional tone that disregards the divine dimension and approaches the biblical narratives and the hymnography as if they were dramatic stories taken from everyday life. We cannot extricate ourselves from the process, as if the continuous transfiguration within the church were a magical process that does not demand our personal participation, and therefore we cannot deny a certain emotional depth in liturgical services, but the fullness of the services is not in our emotions. We may cry, we may rejoice, we may respond in many ways to the continuous drama of Jesus Christ as we relive it in the church. Yet, if we look clearly, we'll realize that our emotions dance next to the abyss of heaven. The Eucharistic sacrament is a change that makes the entire universe shudder throughout its many-billion-light-years diameter. Heaven opens in front of us like a tent on Mount Thabor and God becomes present—we have no emotions capable of responding to the magnitude of this event. In the Eucharistic change we relive the Transfiguration of Christ at both a personal and a cosmic level.

Perhaps for this reason the best way to consider liturgical life in its full dimensions is to see it as a continuous Transfiguration event, both in reference to the historical, biblical, and theological Transfiguration of Jesus Christ, and also in the context of the experience of the divine light. We do justice to the Eucharistic service only when we treat it with the same awe and reverence with which we would welcome a vision of light.

There have been saints who experienced the unity of the sacrament and the vision. St. Symeon the New Theologian was rather young when he had his first visionary experience, which left him utterly confused. It took him several years to understand and accept what had happened to him. From the little we know about his life, it seems that initially he resisted the calling that resulted from his vision. He tried to put it aside, to live like a "normal person," as if nothing had happened to him. But in the end he could not escape the weight of grace, and he devoted the rest of his life to God as a monk and priest.

St. Symeon saw the divine light every time he celebrated the Divine Liturgy. In this, as well as in other things of his life, he was able to see one through the other—the liturgy through the light and vice versa. Instead of separating them and pondering which of the two was superior to the other, he understood that both revealed something about each other. It was difficult for St. Symeon to serve in the altar and not see the Eucharistic meal as a continuous revelation of the glory of God, but it was equally impossible for him to separate the strong sense of the kingdom of God made present in the here and now in his church from the vision of the divine light.

Perhaps because he lived all his life in the divine light, St. Symeon had interesting insights regarding the contrast between sanctity and communion, vision and gathering, ascetic struggle and the Eucharist. He pictured the church as a connection between heaven and earth, using the metaphor of a golden chain.[18] Adding a twist to the ancient metaphor, however, he spoke not of one, but of two golden chains. The first consists of bishops and Eucharistic communities that trace their origin to the apostles and the Lord's Supper. Every ring is locked and guided by the previous ring; every generation is born by the previous generation. In the end, the uninterrupted celebration of the Eucharistic meal means that we partake of the one and only Lord's Supper. Without this beacon that burns without interruption, we would not have the Bible, the theological deliberations of the Fathers, or the doctrine of the Trinity; we would not understand anything about the divine plan of salvation to which God invites us: plainly put, we would not have Christianity.

The saints of the church form the other golden chain. Many of them are unknown to us. But their sacrifice, their grace, their prayer, and their presence give life to the church. In them we can see the church not as an institution, but as a living and breathing body: the mystical, luminous body of Christ. Sanctity in the church is not cultivated or taught with words, with teachings, or even with acts. While words can describe sanctity, more often they can describe what it is not. Acts of love, charity, and self-sacrifice may pour out of it. But in the end, we never get to know anyone by description or even by observing their actions. We get to know a new friend by being with him, by talking to him rather than about him, by doing things with him instead of standing back in order to see what he does, by agreeing and disagreeing, by fighting and reconciling with him, by asking and giving forgiveness, by anticipating him, by being surprised by him, by loving him; in short, by sharing part of our life with him.

It is the same thing with saints, God, and us. It is through the saints of the church that we can feel the breath of the Holy Spirit. The fire of the Holy Spirit is something lived and witnessed, and passed on to others. The church lives in its saints because every saint has received of the sanctity of someone else before them. Saints somehow sense and recognize each other, and in this way they lock as rings in the continuous golden chain, but they also give freely their sanctity to everyone around them. Without the uninterrupted tradition of the saints—if we did not know that in all times throughout the Christian world there were and are saints in whom lives the incarnate and Transfigured Christ—the church would become inert and barren.

Saints are not illuminated people in the sense with which we usually understand this expression. Instead, in reality, the more saintly a person is, the more his personal traits become inconsequential, as if a part of them withdraws in order to make space for the Holy Spirit. Christianity is a religion based on the cult of saints—in liturgical tradition we pray to saints, we ask them to pray for us, we decorate our churches and our homes with icons of saints. Yet, in a paradoxical way, Christianity has no space for the cult of personality. The spiritual model that saints provide is less about a heroic admiration of an important or skillful person, as it is a hope that we may be saved as they were, despite ourselves.

The saints and ascetics who were given the blessing of the vision of the light, the blessing of the tearful prayer, the gift of discernment, the gift of healing, or other blessings of the Holy Spirit were granted this because they turned away from themselves and toward God. For this reason, without a strong connection to the Eucharistic gathering, the cult of saints is meaningless. The vision of the divine light of God is not an end in itself. As in the Transfiguration narrative, what inevitably follows is the return to the world.

In the end, the two golden chains that St. Symeon the New Theologian talked about suggest the same thing. They both describe the church from two different but equally important angles: the church as apostolic and Eucharistic, and also as vivified by the breath of the Holy Spirit. The church is formed around the altar table of Christ, but is also led by the Holy Spirit into the arms of the Father and the kingdom of heaven.

We can approach the question of the tension between the solitary visionary experience and the Eucharistic gathering in a similar way. In antiquity and early Christianity the word *mystical* used to refer, almost exclusively, to rites and rituals. The word that Greek Christianity uses for "sacrament" is actually the word *mysterion,* "mystery." A *mystes* or mystic was the person who was guiding people through their initiation—a priest. The meaning of the words *mystery* and *mystical* is rooted in liturgical service that conveyed something that mere words could not convey. For this reason the interpretations of the Divine Liturgy often describe it as a way of representing the Christological drama and the kingdom of heaven.

It was only after the twelfth century or so that "mystical" broke out of its original context and became connected to the ecstatic or visionary experience. Yet many medieval texts are often read as if they describe the individual experience of the divine (such as the incomparable *Mystical Theology* of Dionysios the Areopagite, written in the sixth century and often studied in the context of the mystical experience). Instead, these texts speak about liturgical services and rituals, and the ascent of the church to God. The new meaning of *mystical,* inaccurate as it may be and filled with theological problems, bears with it a truly spiritual demand: that the church not lose its tangible connection with the Transfigured Christ. That in every Eucharistic gathering we remember the depth and the extent of the revelation of God. That the Eucharist manifests itself to the saints of the church as the same light that shone from the face of Jesus Christ in the mountain of the Transfiguration.

Toward the end of the Divine Liturgy of St. John Chrysostom or St. Basil the Great, the people sing, "We have seen the true light, we have received the heavenly Spirit!" Likewise, when we read or we hear of the magnificent experience of the divine light that transfigured and awakened the spiritual senses of St. Symeon the New Theologian, St. Seraphim of Sarov, or Elder Paisios, we remember that these saints, and the many unknown saints of the past and the present, were given the grace exactly because they made the sacramental presence of Christ the center of their lives. Through their radiance they transfigured the people around them into a communion of saints.

6

TELL NO ONE UNTIL THE SON OF MAN HAS RISEN FROM THE DEAD

Transfiguration and Resurrection

I F WE HAD TO CHOOSE ONE EVENT FROM THE LIFE of Christ as an entry point to explain Christianity, we would look to his Resurrection. I am an Easterner, and it is generally (and stereotypically!) said that the Eastern Church places more emphasis on the Resurrection of Jesus Christ, whereas the West focuses on his Incarnation. As with many stereotypical positions, this is not completely true and yet we cannot dismiss it easily. As the Greeks say, "Where there is smoke, there is fire!"

Growing up in Greece, I learned about the Easter or Pascha feast as a part of the wider culture, even as Orthodox Easter as celebrated in the West is far bigger than a one-day event. In the Orthodox Church, a few minutes before midnight on Easter Sunday we find a church that is full. In addition to the people inside the church, we'll often see twice as many people standing outside, holding their candles and lamps, waiting to hear the hymn that announces the good news of the Resurrection of Christ: "Christ is risen from the dead."

Usually only the first word is heard, because immediately afterward, a torrential noise of fireworks and bells, lasting for many minutes, drowns out the rest of the words. It is a noise so excessive that you would think it could follow up on the theme of the Resurrection and wake the dead. In the celebration, everyone embraces and kisses the people around them, whether they are family members or people they have never seen before.

That is a glimpse of the first few moments of Easter, but Easter actually lasts much longer. Forty days before the Holy Week, we get into preparation mode, at the beginning of Lent. The decorations and colors in the church change, and the services themselves change. Instead of the liturgy of St. John Chrysostom, on Lent Sundays we celebrate the slightly longer liturgy of St. Basil. More services are added to the weekly schedule, such as the Pre-sanctified Vesperal Liturgy, the Salutations to the Mother of God, and the Akathist. The Psalter, which is read liturgically each week of the year in monasteries and parishes that observe a rigorous liturgical program, is now read twice within a week. The fast is rigorous: no meat, fish, dairy, or eggs are eaten for seven weeks (and except for Saturdays and Sundays not even oil or alcohol are consumed). Many people find that they cannot follow this strict program, but even those who do not observe it fully can sense the difference in the air.

Then we come to Holy Week, when everyone, even people who are not particularly religious, goes to church. The dramatic and long service of the twelve Passion Gospels on the night of Holy Thursday is followed by the Epitaphios, a service that is no less than the funeral of Christ, when all the people follow a flower-studded canopy with the image of Christ taken to his grave and process through their neighborhood, every neighborhood and every parish with their own Epitaphios. Although this is a solemn procession, it is far from macabre and depressing. The fragrance of the incense, combined with the smells of nature in spring, intensifies the anticipation for the celebration that everyone knows is just around the corner. The melodies of the funeral hymns of the Epitaphios are solemn and pleasant and known by all, religious or not alike. Then, after the celebration on the night of the Resurrection, which ends with a rich and heavy meal at around three AM, a weeklong celebration starts, known as Renewal Week—the week following the renewal of the world.

The Events of the Gospel in Reverse Order—Resurrection First

As a child I knew that Easter meant two weeks off school, but a lot of that time was spent in church. In total, the Easter event, which in all its extensions (Lent, Holy Week, Renewal Week) lasts about sixty days, is one sixth of the entire year. The celebration of Easter and the Resurrection of Christ is not just a theological event or something for only pious Christians. My childhood memories of the celebration tell me much more about the Resurrection of Jesus Christ than a theological book on the subject ever could. But then, this is exactly what we hope liturgical life does: translate the good news of the Resurrection and the presence of Christ among us in a way that can be felt and internalized by all.

While the other Christological events and feasts of the church reveal something necessary about Jesus Christ and the salvation he offers, the work of Christ and our salvation would not be carried out without his full Incarnation and without the establishment, in his person, of the only link known between the uncreated God and humanity. We know no other such complete link between God and the world. It is important, therefore, to realize the full extent of the Incarnation, and internalize it spiritually through the Feast of the Nativity. Every event in the life of Christ, as it is presented in the Gospels, is important. The Baptism of Jesus Christ, the Annunciation to his mother, his selection of the twelve apostles, his healings, his sermons, the Mystical Supper, everything has its place in our spiritual and worship tradition. Nothing is superfluous. But from a certain perspective, which characterizes the early church and the East, it is in the Resurrection that the whole work of Christ comes together. For this reason it can be helpful to consider the narratives of the gospel backward, as if it were starting from the Resurrection of Jesus Christ and proceeding to his Crucifixion, his teachings and his Nativity. Then, in full anticipation of the Passion and the Resurrection that we know has happened, we can appreciate the organic and dynamic relationship of many of the events in the life of Christ. This is certainly the case with the Transfiguration.

My own background, my own experiences in the Orthodox Church, help me extend backward the significance, or rather the prominence, of Easter and the Resurrection of Christ, and see that something similar was happening in the early church. In the early church the Resurrection of Christ was not just the most prominent feast; in some ways it was the only feast of the church.[19]

Yet the significance of the Resurrection in the early church is not limited to the antiquity of its celebration. It is true that in the annual festal cycle the Resurrection of Christ is celebrated sometime in the spring, when the natural light prevails over darkness,[20] but in addition, every Sunday is also a celebration of the Resurrection of Jesus Christ. We see this in the triumphant character of the Sunday liturgy (an ancient church canon from the First Ecumenical Council, for instance, dictates that we should not kneel on the Sunday liturgy, because it is the day of the Resurrection), we can see this in the service of Matins in the East: Matins (or Orthros, in Greek) includes a Gospel reading, almost always related to the Resurrection of Christ.

The connection of the Resurrection and the Sunday liturgy, however, runs even deeper than any historical and liturgical arguments. Since the time of earliest Christianity, since the time of the catacombs, what draws Christians together for their common liturgical worship is the Eucharistic bread and wine. What makes the Eucharist the focal point, the center of reference and the source of the Christian life, is that in a way we cannot explain, it is the body and the blood of Christ: the *resurrected* body and blood of Christ, which knows no physical limitations. The Resurrection of Christ is the theological and liturgical basis for the Eucharistic act. A prayer from the liturgy of St Basil includes this phrase of St Paul: "As often as you eat this bread and drink this cup, you proclaim the Lord's death till he comes" (1 Cor. 11:26). Bringing this idea to completion, the text of the liturgy adds, "and you confess my resurrection." The word *confess* here falls short of describing how the church lives and participates in the death and Resurrection of Jesus Christ.

It is often said among theologians that if we want to look for the sine qua non of the church, the element that defines it and cannot be understood without it, we would point to the Eucharistic meal, which in some way manifests the real presence of Christ in the church. And the church is also living in anticipation of the full advent of the kingdom of heaven, the resurrection of the dead, and the Second Coming of Christ in glory. These are some of the aspects of Christianity that cannot be ignored when we try to understand what the church and its Eucharistic center are.

When I try to describe the church and the Eucharist with definitions and explanations, I realize that I just cannot do it properly. Sometimes people ask me about spiritual matters and how they are taken in the church, or what informs our attitude on social issues or issues of justice and faith, and the best answer I can give is "come and see." These are the same words that Philip told Nathanael in John 1:46, when the latter wondered how it was possible for the Messiah to have come from Nazareth. This "come and see" is a source of responsibility and a source of joy. Even before I tried to think about these things, when my mind and my heart were simply absorbing what they would encounter, I could sense that the moment of Eucharistic communion was one in which the whole universe stopped and bowed in front of the love and sacrifice of Christ who condescended to be there, in a humble chalice. Sometimes we have moments when we can really see and realize where you are. The moment itself, in which the Holy Spirit can show us the breadth of the heavens, is the intensification and the focal point of all that Christ ever was, is, and will be—creation, resurrection, and restoration in the kingdom of God all at once. It is through that touch that we can hear the breathing of the saints and we can hear the heart of the church beating.

Scripture, in the words of St. Paul, recognized the Resurrection as the basis of the entire Christian faith in 1 Corinthians 15:14–15: "If

Christ is not risen, then our preaching is empty and your faith is also empty. Yes, and we are found false witnesses of God, because we have testified of God that he raised up Christ." And the Eucharist is the way the church experiences and participates in the Resurrection of Christ continuously.

Rather than a conceptual, abstract, or mental resurrection (such as the hope that our name or our memory will remain in the world even after our death), the full meaning of the Eucharistic body of Christ is based on a leap of existence. Do I realize I am already dead? Do I realize that although I may walk, talk, write, and think, all this is no different than a projection of a shadow to a wall, and that life is elsewhere? I realize this only to some extent. But when I do, as if in a moment when I feel completely alone, if I get up in the dark house in the middle of the night, I realize that there is a deeper truth, a more real reality and existence, to which I can turn.

I cannot do this by thinking my way out of the darkness, and I cannot do it merely by trying to prepare myself for a judgment of my actions and justification of my mistakes. Neither thought nor self-control can get me out of the tomb. It is by placing myself in the event of the one and only Resurrection that I can escape death.

The Eucharistic body of Christ is not a magic spell that will cure me by miracle, but it is there so that I can become it. Eucharistic communion is not an activity that comes from the outside. We do not eat the bread and drink the wine to receive automatic salvation as if a drug entered our body, attacked the cells of the virus, and restored our health—if it were that simple, the whole world would have escaped the effects of sin.

I eat the bread and drink the wine because I want to become the bread and wine—to be, as these two things, a participant of the Resurrection of Christ, a member of his Resurrected body. This is because when I say Christ in this context, I am referring to the Resurrected Christ, the one who is not an individual, but the underpinnings of life and existence anywhere, who stares me in the face. For the church, for the transformative power that allows me to touch that which is life, existence, and freedom, I start with the real presence of Christ in his dead and living saints; I start with the Eucharistic real presence. And when anyone asks me to explain this, I can only say "come and see."

Resurrection and Transfiguration

It is difficult for us to visualize how our own self may become a Eucharistic, Christified body. Our eyes are not enough here, because they only know how to look, and not to see.

The Transfiguration of Jesus Christ offered this glorified state as a model for our own glorification, our own hope of becoming part of the body of Christ. This is not easy to put into words or to understand rationally, but what the eyes cannot see, the soul can sense in a different way. And what it can sense is something that has been given to us in Scripture: the close connection between the Transfiguration of Christ and his Resurrected body passes through the Eucharistic chalice.

If I try to throw myself and my whole existence to the feet of Christ, who showed with his Resurrection that he is the source of any kind of life-force we may imagine, then I can only imagine my final destination as a destination of a body of light. I must submit my own existence to the love of God given to his own creatures, whom he keeps in life with his continuous breath, so that I too may become as much alive as that tiny piece of bread soaked in wine. It is no bigger than a spoonful, but the Eucharist contains and exceeds the life-force of the entire universe. This body, the same as it was given to me, now infused in the divine rays that permeate it and change it. Our own resurrection is not so much, or at least not only, the resurrection of all the dead, righteous and wicked, at the end of time. Our resurrection, our union with the source of our life, is more properly understood according to the image of the Transfiguration of Christ, and our own transfiguration in him.

To put it in other words, the person who shares in the Resurrection of Christ becomes a human Eucharist, in a transfiguration that follows the Transfigured, glorified Christ. And in doing so, in becoming the Eucharistic body of the one Christ, we meet everyone else who also has been transfigured in Christ.

Still, the Resurrection of Jesus Christ from the dead is a mystery that our mind cannot process fully. The Gospels do not describe the historical Resurrection of Christ, and yet the words *gospel* or *evangelion* (good news) refer to the good news of the Resurrection of Christ from the dead. But even the disciples of Christ found it difficult to grasp this great mystery, the cornerstone of the Christian faith. The early church dedicated many hymns and sermons to the Resurrection of Christ, but it took several centuries until artists tried their hand at a representation of the Resurrected Christ. And then, how did they do that? They used the image of the Transfiguration as a model.

The Transfigured Christ in the Icon of Resurrection

In early Christianity iconography was taken very seriously since an entire ecumenical council in the eighth century was dedicated to the use of icons in worship. Icons are shaped by theological thought, prayer, and church practice. They also influence, with their presence, theological thought, prayer, and church practice. Icons are placed in churches or homes because they carry a presence about them. In a limited, symbolic, or partial way, an icon of Christ is a presence of Christ. For all intents and purposes we can approach icons with the same reverence that we approach sermons, teachings, and doctrines. With that understanding, what do we see if we compare the icon of the Resurrection and the icon of the Transfiguration, which preceded it by at least three centuries?

Both icon types focus on the figure of Jesus Christ, whose garments are white. The Transfiguration narrative specifies that the color of the garments of Jesus was resplendent white, and the only other bit of biblical information we have about what he had ever worn is about the clean shroud that Joseph of Arimathea provided, which may indeed have also been white. What Jesus wears in the icon of the Resurrection is not a burial shroud, however, it is a garment of glory, the same kind of garment he wore on Mount Thabor.

Likewise, the light and the splendor that came from the face of Jesus, which shone brighter than the sun, are represented in the icon of the Transfiguration with a luminous aureole that surrounds the body of Christ. We see the same aureole in the icon of the Resurrection, although there is nothing in the written sources to suggest a miracle of light. What we do understand from these two similarities is that the Resurrected Christ of iconography is the same as the Christ of the icon of the Transfiguration.[21]

Consider this from another angle. Every resurrection, even the ones that were performed before the Resurrection of Christ, such as the raising of Lazarus and the raising of the daughter of Jairus, or even miracles of resurrection that can be found in the Old Testament, such as Elijah's raising of the son of the widow in 1 Kings 17, draws its meaning from the Resurrection of Christ—we say this because only in the person of Christ do we find the complete connection between heaven and earth, the world and life. But in the event of the Transfiguration we can already see how the limits of life and death do not apply to Christ. He summons Moses and Elijah from wherever they were (although the usual reading of Scripture suggests that Elijah may have never died, technically speaking, the book of Deuteronomy ends with the death of Moses), showing that Jesus is the master of life and death. The presence of Moses and Elijah may not be thought of as a resurrection in the usual way we think of this miracle, yet it demonstrates the power of Christ over death.

The choice of the glorious image of the Transfigured Christ as a model for the development of the icon of the Resurrection was a striking and inspired choice, and it shows that the Resurrection of Christ is deeply related with his Transfiguration. If we imagine the scene of the historical Resurrection of Jesus Christ, most likely what will come to our mind is the image of a resplendent Jesus emerging from the tomb while the soldiers who guard the tomb fall flat on the ground, too terrified to even raise their eyes and see him. Or perhaps we may think of the Eastern imagery of the Resurrection, where a resplendent Jesus steps on the broken gates of Hades and raises Adam and Eve. Both these images, however (at least speaking strictly from a visual point of view), were given to us not because of a description of the Resurrection in the Gospels, apocryphal writings, or early Christian writings, but because it made sense for early Christians to look at the only biblical description of Jesus appearing in glory, in full manifestation of his divinity, as a means of representing the moment of his Resurrection from the dead.

Apart from the visual connection, the preference of the Eastern Christian Church to associate, iconographically, the Resurrection of Christ with his descent to Hades, says something very important for the Resurrection and the Transfiguration. Looking carefully at this image, we realize that it does not portray the emergence of Christ from the tomb, but the raising of Adam and Eve from their tomb. Instead of the historical Resurrection of Jesus Christ, what the icon shows us is the eternal resurrection of the church by Christ.

The Feast of Tabernacles and the Resurrection of the Church

And then there is something else we come across in the person of the Resurrected and Transfigured Christ that explains the biblical narrative and the importance of the white clothes of Jesus. The biblical text alludes to a connection between the Transfiguration and the Feast of the Tabernacles, which is supported by historical evidence.[22] This connection became less significant in Christianity, as it moved quickly beyond its Hebrew context, and for this reason it is no more than an allusion in the Gospels.

The three tents that Peter proposed to erect refer to the Feast of the Tabernacles, which is still celebrated as it was at the time of Jesus, by setting up tents. In the narratives of Matthew, Mark, and Luke, the Transfiguration follows after Peter's confession of faith, but in John's Gospel the confession is followed by the Feast of the Tabernacles. The context is there.

During the Feast of the Tabernacles in the time of Jesus, the high priest wore resplendent white vestments. This was received in messianic overtones, because in earlier times the Feast of the Tabernacles reserved a special role for the king of Israel. As Israel did not have a king at the time of Jesus, the high priest carried upon himself his memory and a hopeful anticipation for his return in the future. Therefore, the emergence of the high priest from the temple in white vestments was a ritual expectation of the Messiah. In this context the change of the color of the garments of Jesus in the biblical text identifies him as the Messiah, or more precisely, as the high priest who fulfils the messianic expectations of the people.

Why was Jesus being identified as a high priest? What priestly act did he perform? His role as the spiritual Messiah, which he stresses several times in the Bible, is to lead the people toward a spiritual, rather than a political, liberation. His liberation is one that leads to God. On Mount Thabor Christ demonstrates this by showing the kingdom of heaven to Peter, John, and James, by giving a new meaning to the Feast of the Tabernacles. More precisely, the Transfiguration of Christ is the fulfillment of the Feast of the Tabernacles—following what he said in Matthew 5:17, where Jesus explains that he came to fulfill the law. The symbolism and the imagery of the Transfiguration show how this fulfillment is the transformation of the anticipation and the expectation that we find in the Old Testament, into the presence of Christ and the recognition of the salvation he brings.

Moreover, the image of Christ as the Messiah and high priest, as foretold and prepared by the Old Testament and manifested in the Transfiguration, helps us penetrate into the image of the Resurrection. We see a different act that also flows from the priesthood of Christ: the resurrection of the church. As we see in the Orthodox icon of the Resurrection, which taught us to look at the resurrected Jesus as the glorified Messiah and high priest of the Transfiguration, Christ raises the fallen humanity and leads it to the kingdom of heaven.

In all of these images, the Transfiguration is the key by which we can unlock and understand the Resurrection of Christ, as much as this is possible. The most obvious direct connection between the two events is given in the Gospels of Mark and Matthew. In both of them, Christ asks Peter, John, and James to say nothing about what they just witnessed, "until the Son of Man is risen from the dead." Why did he ask them this? How could they have possibly understood this request for secrecy? And what can this possibly mean for us, who receive the word of God today and hope to be saved by it?

The Transfiguration and the Resurrection of Jesus were connected by a bond of silence on the way down from the mountain of the Transfiguration. This bond of silence implies that their connection is beyond words, and that by placing the one next to the other we can understand something beyond the narrative. In other words, our resurrection in Jesus Christ and eternal life in God implies that we are transfigured by the Transfiguration of Christ, that we allow the grace of God to fill us with his light.

All this certainly sounds overwhelming. There is a lot to reflect on here, many theological and spiritual connections to make, and much to consider in the context of history and typology. But perhaps this is why we can think of the Transfiguration of Christ as a revelation of divinity and an invitation to his Resurrection. Divinity reveals itself in riddles, enigmas, and entry points that invite us to penetrate deeper and deeper into its mystery—but in the end, our journey depends on what God does.

There is a good reason for this. This continuous hide-and-seek with God engages us in a lifelong quest for discovery, but ultimately it is not a journey of knowledge. Every word, ritual, or symbol brings us closer to God by taking us away from words, rituals, and symbols. If we think of the extent of this ascent toward God, we may be disheartened, because the distance is impossible to cover. Within the limitations of our nature, we have no more hope of reaching God than a mad boatman in the night who hopes to row all the way to the moon that is reflected on the water. And yet, the miracle of the Transfiguration shows us that the grace of God covers the distance. It is as if the moon takes pity on the mad boatman and makes the miracle by sending its rays to lift him. Similarly, Christ and the Holy Spirit cover the distance, lifting us toward God, even if the distance will never be covered. As we reflect increasingly on what the revelation of the Trinity on Mount Thabor meant, we juxtapose continuously the image of the Transfiguration next to the image of the Resurrection: beyond a first level of symbolism and revelation, there is very little difference between the transfiguration of our nature and our continuous resurrection in Jesus Christ. The question is, how do we live this transfiguration in our daily life?

Living Transfigured Lives Today

Although the Transfiguration was a complete revelation of the Divinity, the three frightened disciples who witnessed it were only able to partially participate in it. For them, as well as for us who see the Transfiguration through their eyes and the narratives that were written after their testimony, full participation implies sharing in the death and Resurrection of Christ.

Paul writes to the Romans about the grace that gives eternal life, but only after he has told them in the beginning of the sixth chapter about the death of Christ, which we participate in as well. How do we do this? Is it as simple as trying to be a good person who leads a moral life? A lot of what we find in the Bible and in the tradition of the church is about following the commandments of God, which encourages this kind of reading, but we also find countless examples where one moment of true and complete repentance can weigh much more than an entire life of sin.

Morality is about things that are done that should not be done, and about things that are not done that should be done. It starts with behavior and actions, although thoughts may be included as well. But morality goes deeper than thoughts or actions. A moral person is one whose good actions reflect a good and honest heart. You do not have to be a Christian to be a good person. Social conscience, respect of the rights of others, love for humanity, and a sense of honesty and decency are qualities that can be shared by people of all religions, and even by people with no religious or metaphysical background. While many Christians base their moral compass in Jesus Christ and the God of love, it is hard to say whether Christians are better people than non-Christians. In the end, although such a life is a good thing, it is not enough for our salvation.

The aim of the Christian life is not social harmony or a just life, but union with God. The example of the Pharisees, which is brought up several times in the Gospels, is very revealing. For all we know, the Pharisees, who were largely preoccupied with a moral code of rules, actually observed the rules they were preaching. For all we know, most of them could have been strict interpreters of Scripture, which they used as a basis for their actions. Surely a person no less than Paul, who was a Pharisee before he was blinded and illuminated by the light of God on the way to Damascus, was no hypocrite as a Pharisee. But the strong words with which Christ consistently attacks the Pharisees show that it was not the few bad apples that he was criticizing but the entire approach of turning the relationship of God with his people from a living, dynamic thing into a code of regulations.

The law of God served to train humanity to the ways of divine love, and the presence of Christ makes it obsolete. The wish of God is not to judge, but to save the world. God desires to fill the world with his grace, to call all beings into a free relationship of love. Life loves what is alive, and God loves what is free, and he loves us unconditionally. The foremost command or wish of God, that passionate lover of humankind who knows no bounds in his love for us, is not to obey him, but to love him.

The relationship of the church and God has been described in countless texts. In the Song of Songs it is described as a relationship of deep love. God may be above all passions and necessities, but we recognize in him only one strong passion: his intense love for humankind. Words such as covenant and testament that have been used to describe the relationship between God and the people are sometimes understood in a legal framework—as contracts between two mutually bound parties—but it is more precise to understand them in a nuptial context, as if we are speaking about the marital contract, the confirmation and proclamation of love between God and the church. We understand this dynamic much better when we think of God as the lover of humanity rather than as its judge.

What exists between two spouses is more than the sum of the parts. Mutual respect, distinct roles, equal responsibilities, all these are things that are very important, but we can appreciate how little they are if we imagine a cold nightmare of a dialogue between two spouses, the kind that nobody wants to experience. The man might say, "In twenty years I never cheated on you, I never insulted you, I never raised my voice. You kept the property you had before our wedding, and I kept mine. I did everything an honest husband is supposed to do. Why do you now want to leave me?" It would be terrible if the wife could answer simply, "This is right. You did all that. There is no flaw in anything you did. But you never loved me either. Seeing your wife as a responsibility is not enough."

Love between spouses is based on a death and a transfiguration. When two lovers are united with each other, they try to make space inside them for the other. The paradox of the act of love is that the man and the woman fulfill and negate their gender at the same time. Sexuality brings them together, but at its culmination they have submitted their gender to each other. Making love is a "covenant" between the two lovers where they agree to give themselves to each other completely and unconditionally. This communion of the man and the woman is a death, a transfiguration, and a new existence. At its culmination the two individuals stop being themselves—orgasm is a moment of surrender, a little death. They exist in a different way, even if for a brief moment, liberated from the bonds of individuality. In this new being, which is held together only by the covenant of love, they share their difference with the other person. The result is a shared existence that includes sexual differentiation, but ultimately transcends it and is fulfilled at the level of the human being beyond this differentiation. And although we may point to the lovemaking as the act that gives meaning to the relationship of the man and the woman, they carry this dynamic in their life even beyond the conjugal bed.

The metaphor of love can also describe the dynamic relationship between humanity and God. If our relationship with God is similar to the love between a man and a woman, we can read the Christological drama and the economy of salvation as an act of love: God died in order to become fully like us, in order to give us the space we need to die in him as well. To die according to nature, as we do when we are baptized, is not a negation of the human condition, just as the sharing of the lovers is a fulfillment rather than a negation of their sexual identity. We need to die as individuals in order to form symbiotic pairs. We are not a species that can live on its own. Gender dimorphism implies that a man is incomplete without a woman, because he cannot embrace the entire human condition (at least according to nature) on his own. If we discover a new insect with male sexual organs, we assume that the female of the species also exists, even if we have not seen it yet. Similarly, from a larger point of view, human nature is meaningless on its own; it can only survive in a symbiotic relation with God. Death in God means that we save our humanity by offering it to him. We accept to die as individuals, we liberate our nature from the confines of individuality, in order to live a life in God. In this way we share his Resurrection and we receive eternal life—his life.

Our Transfiguration into Christ through the Eucharist

If making love is the act that gives meaning to the relationship of a man and a woman, the act that gives meaning to our relationship with God is the Eucharist. There is an important difference, however. While human love involves two lovers, the love of God involves the entire church. The Eucharist is the place where we meet and are united not only with Christ, but also with everyone else who wishes to be so united—with the entire church. This suggests that our transfiguration in Christ is not an individual one, but a transfiguration of the many into one, of the people who make up the body of the church into the body of Christ. As the corporate body of Christ we live his entire life, which is symbolically laid out in the Eucharist.

Our transfiguration leads us to become human Eucharistic hosts ourselves. We participate in the life of Christ when we become the consecrated bread and wine; when our body becomes the body of Christ—not only the historical or the ecclesial body of Christ, but his sacramental body, sanctified by the bonds of love between us and God. Our body is broken when the bread is broken, it is pierced when the bread is pierced by the lance, and it is raised to the cross when the bread is raised. Our transfiguration changes us to Christological beings, and we live all the stages of salvation that Christ inaugurated for us.

This is where we begin to share in his Crucifixion and his Resurrection. And when the Holy Spirit changes the bread and the wine, it also changes us because we have accepted the will of God for ourselves, as Christ himself accepted the will of the Father in the Mount of Olives. It is not the thing-ness of the bread that changes us (there is no religious magic), but the real presence of the Trinity grasps us from the bottom of our existence and raises us to the kingdom of God. If we accept and acquiesce to this divine push that takes us over the heavens, how can we not give up the individual resistances that keep us separated from God? And, if when we become the bread and the wine, we also meet there everyone else who offered themselves as lambs participating in the sacrifice of the one Lamb, if we see that the glow of Christ has transfigured the teacher, the public servant, the butcher, and the carpenter, how can we not love them too, as the second command Christ says, like ourself? Perhaps this is exactly the greatest practical difference between seeing the ascent to God as a moral struggle and seeing it as a trajectory of transfiguration: in the grace of the transfiguration we can discern, marvel, and rejoice with the change of others into the body of Christ. If we find ourselves surrounded by saints and angels, or if we recognize the saint in everyone around us, that means that we are already in the kingdom of God.

The Crucifixion and the Resurrection of Christ cannot be separated. They are not really two distinct events, but are two parts of the same act of salvation. Both at the level of the church and at the personal level, they express what St. Paul writes in his letter to the Galatians: "I have been crucified with Christ; it is no longer I who live, but Christ lives in me; and the life which I now live in the flesh I live by faith in the Son of God, who loved me and gave himself for me" (Gal. 2:20). What was done once and for all by Christ becomes our life by our continuous transfiguration into his church.

The mystery of the Crucifixion and the Resurrection of the church is that we are transformed from fallen individuals, subject to necessity, pain, anger, jealousy, and all the passions that keep us imprisoned inside our own skin, into participants of the freedom and the eternity of God. To do this, we live according to what we learned in our baptism: in order to be raised with Christ as members of his body, we first have to participate in his death, to die with him. This means that we willingly embrace our physical death and we turn our eyes elsewhere, into what is beyond. Life is elsewhere. In order to invite the eternal God inside us, we need to make space for him first. The Crucifixion, as the last public image of Christ on the earth, invites Christians to start their ascent to him through their participation in his Cross.

This is very difficult. And in this context, the Transfiguration is a guide for our salvation through the Cross and the Resurrection. The splendor of the body of Christ is a promise and a revelation of our own future with Christ. But this is only the model. It won't become real until we pass through the Cross and the Tomb. The glory of Christ is not something that is given as a thing we can possess and hold on to, but it is a complete transformation, a transfiguration of human nature. If the Crucifixion is the last public image of Jesus Christ on earth and the beginning of our death and resurrection in Christ, the Transfiguration, as the luminous image of Christ in glory, is the best approximation we have for its conclusion. It is, perhaps, the most accurate memory the church has of Christ, having passed through his death and Resurrection, having been baptized with him, and having accepted him to be born inside us. This is the memory and the image of Christ in his fullness, above life and death, as the doorway to the kingdom of heaven, the brilliance of the Father, revealed by the Holy Spirit, resting in his saints, and inviting us into his brightness.

We embark on this journey of divine discovery by placing ourselves on Mount Thabor with the fallen disciples of Jesus. They saw their Master in his divinity so that they could understand something more about who he was, and thus they would be better prepared to face his forthcoming

Passion and Resurrection. By showing to them his power and his glory, Christ told them essentially this: "This is who I really am. You'll see me beaten, tortured, and crucified. You'll see me die on a cross. But nature and death cannot restrict me. I'll rise from the dead. I'll be as glorious and as luminous as you see me now. When I come back at the end of time, I will also be as you see me now, bathed in the light of my divinity. Until I return, remember my life, but me as you see me now. Every time you need to remember that time, space, and death has no power over me, every time you need to remember that what I give you is the union of the complete nature of humanity with the complete nature of God, you can remember me as I appear now in front of you, surrounded by the prophets of old who were brought here to see me and talk with me, brighter than the sun, singled out and recognized by my Father for who I am, for your sake. This is the mystery of my Transfiguration. And if you want to follow me, you'll die many times and you'll be raised with me many times, but what you see right now will be your guidance, the compass in your death, and the promise of eternal life."

1. Editor's Note: *Metamorphosis: The Transfiguration in Byzantine Theology and Iconography*, by Andreas Andreopoulos (Crestwood, NY: St. Vladimir's Seminary Press, 2005).

2. Edwin Muir, "The Transfiguration" from *The Labyrinth*, in *Collected Poems 1921–1958*, (London: Faber & Faber, 1960).

3. A good discussion of the biblical themes in the narrative of the Transfiguration can be found in Dorothy Lee, *Transfiguration* (New York: Continuum, 2004).

4. This is made evident by the fact that both glory (δόξα) and majesty (μεγαλειότης) render the same concept, which in Hebrew is expressed by the word *kabod*.

5. The word δόξα, which is normally translated as "glory," has a very different meaning in Greek before its use by the translation of the Old Testament to Greek in the third century *bc*, known as Septuagint, which uses it for the first time in this sense, trying to render the Hebrew words *kabod* and *shekinah*, or the Aramaic *yekara*. These words suggest "the presence of God," and glory as it is used in the context of the New Testament often means this as well. Δόξα in Platonic Greek, for instance, means "opinion," or "subjective view," but also can refer to the departure point for a deeper discovery, in which we pass from subjective opinion to a grasp of reality beyond words. It is an extremely interesting question why the Septuagint translators chose a word with a very different meaning when they needed to render the concept of *kabod*, which could have been

approximated more closely with a word such as theophany. One way to see this is that the presence of God could not be defined by a word, but only by a way of discovery. Nevertheless, the choice of a word that suggests a personal involvement or participation in, or perhaps a leap of faith for the discovery of the presence of God, says something about how the presence of God was understood in the Old Testament. What we see here is something very similar to the way the Gospel of Luke refers to the kingdom of God in chapter 17, verses 20–21, which shows that the way to the kingdom is an inward path: "when he was asked by the Pharisees when the kingdom of God would come, he answered them and said, 'The kingdom of God does not come with observation; nor will they say, 'See here!' or 'See there!' For indeed, the kingdom of God is within you.'"

6. Cf. Andreopoulos, *Metamorphosis*, 56–60, for a discussion of these views.

7. Although different translations of the Bible in English use different words, such as "transformed," the Greek word in both passages is μεταμορφούμεθα, a word of the same root as in Mark's and Matthew's narrative of the Transfiguration.

8. The reason the words that are heard in the Baptism of Christ are slightly different in Mark and Luke's version is that they are addressed to Christ ("You are my beloved Son . . . ") and not to the crowd.

9. This is, admittedly, a theological minefield. Eastern and Western Christianity have not seen eye to eye on this for many centuries. Perhaps the difference of opinion regarding the procession of the Holy Spirit is the deepest, most serious difference between them. And yet, the Baptism and the Transfiguration of Christ, as the two biblical events where the presence of the three persons of the

Trinity is evident in these texts, have not been examined fully with an eye to the resolution of this theological difference.

10. This is exemplified beautifully in the Baptism narrative of the Gospel according to Matthew: in Matthew 3:16 we hear that after he "had been baptized, Jesus came up immediately from the water." People who were baptized by John confessed their sins and then they came out. The sinless Jesus, who had nothing to confess, came out of the water immediately.

11. This is a Trinitarian model that we find in several Fathers of the Church in the East, such as Cyril of Alexandria, John of Damascus, and Photios the Great, and was connected with the Orthodox resistance to the Western interpolation of the words "and from the Son" regarding the procession of the Holy Spirit in the Creed. What we see in the Baptism is that the Holy Spirit does not proceed from the Son, but only from the Father.

12. Following the model of Moses, who purified himself and did not sleep with his wife the night before he ascended Sinai, Orthodox priests do not sleep with their wives the night before they celebrate the Divine Liturgy.

13. Maximos the Confessor, *Various Texts on Theology, the Divine Economy, and Virtue and Vice, Second Century*, PG 90, 1244.

14. This story can be found in the fifth volume of the *Golden Legend*, the collection of saints' lives that Jacobus de Voragine compiled in 1275.

15. Although the ascent of Moses is associated with Mount Sinai and the ascent of Elijah with Mount Horeb, it is generally held that these are different names for the same place.

16. Symeon the New Theologian, *The Discourses*, trans. C.J. deCatanzaro (New York: Paulist Press, 1980), 245–46.

17. This testimony was first published in 1903 in Russian, after the death of N. Motovilov who transcribed it. It is reproduced here in an abridged form, from the English translation of Mary-Barbara Zeldin, published in C. Cavarnos and M.-B. Zeldin, *St. Seraphim of Sarov* (Belmont, MA: Institute for Byzantine and Modern Greek Studies, 1980), 93–122.

18. Anticipating the advent of the One God, Homer puts some strange words in the mouth of Zeus in the *Iliad*. Zeus tells the other gods that if they tie him with a golden chain and pull him with it, they won't be able to pull him down to earth. He, on the other hand, the father of gods and mortals, could lift all of them with a single pull. Since then, the golden chain has been used as a symbol of the connection between heaven and earth by pagan and Christian writers.

19. Christmas was instituted as a feast only in the fourth century, and even then not exactly as the celebration of the Incarnation of God, but as the manifestation of the glory of God and his divinity to the world. This meant that it included several other events that could also fit under the umbrella of the "manifestation of the glory of God to the world" but were later separated from the celebration of the Nativity in Bethlehem, such as the Baptism of Christ in the Jordan. In addition, several early theologians did not point to the Nativity of Christ as the moment of his Incarnation, but to the Annunciation and conception of Jesus Christ in the womb of Mary. And whereas the East and the West for some time celebrated the Nativity of Christ on different dates without this ever causing a problem between them, the celebration of Easter was seen as such an important issue that it was one of the things that were fixed in the first meeting of representatives from every part of the Christian Church, the first ecumenical council in Nicea in 325. Even in the West, Easter was the most prominent feast for a long

time, probably until the nineteenth century when in popular imagination Christmas started taking on the weight it still has today. Unfortunately, this was not because the celebration of the Nativity of Jesus Christ and the Incarnation of God was given any further consideration. Although the joviality of the end of December, the tree in our home, the decorations in cities after Thanksgiving, or the dressing of store windows are very pleasant, there is very little that has to do with the Incarnation and the Nativity of Jesus Christ. The Dickens story that in a sense set the tenor for Christmas as a season of good will, solidarity, and social justice makes no reference to the meeting of the eternal and uncreated God with our human nature. And finally, the dominant figure of the season, the fat jolly man in red and white, who came out of the imagination of the marketing department of Coca-Cola, has nothing to do with St. Nicholas, the ascetic bishop whose memory is celebrated earlier that month, or with the Incarnation of Christ. Christmas as a Christian feast has almost but disappeared, or rather its spiritual meaning has been limited among those who seek it actively. Christmas may still be in the hearts of Christians, but it is not in the air anymore.

20. The principle for the date of Easter and the way it is calculated is this: Easter falls the first Sunday (it has to be a Sunday because the whole Holy Week is preparing the day of the Resurrection) after the first full moon after spring equinox. The traditional symbolism, which was passed to Christianity from a similar principle in the date of the Jewish Passover, is that in the spring equinox there is a perfect balance between light and darkness, as the duration of the day is the same as the duration of the night. After that date, the light lasts longer. The full moon tips the balance even more, since even the night is filled with light.

21. Further information about this may be found in Andreopoulos, *Metamorphosis*, 161–67.

22. Further information about this may be found in Harald Riesenfeld, *Jesus Transfiguré: L'Arrière Plan du récit évangelique de la Transfiguration de Notre Seigneur* (ASNU no. 16, Copenhagen, 1947).

ABOUT PARACLETE PRESS

Who We Are

Paraclete Press is a publisher of books, recordings, and DVDs on Christian spirituality. Our publishing represents a full expression of Christian belief and practice—from Catholic to Evangelical, from Protestant to Orthodox.

We are the publishing arm of the Community of Jesus, an ecumenical monastic community in the Benedictine tradition. As such, we are uniquely positioned in the marketplace without connection to a large corporation and with informal relationships to many branches and denominations of faith.

What We Are Doing

Paraclete Press Books Paraclete publishes books that show the richness and depth of what it means to be Christian. Although Benedictine spirituality is at the heart of who we are and all that we do, we publish books that reflect the Christian experience across many cultures, time periods, and houses of worship. We publish books that nourish the vibrant life of the church and its people.

We have several different series, including the best-selling Paraclete Essentials and Paraclete Giants series of classic texts in contemporary English; Voices from the Monastery—men and women monastics writing about living a spiritual life today; our award-winning Paraclete Poetry series as well as the Mount Tabor Books on the arts; best-selling gift books for children on the occasions of baptism and first communion; and the Active Prayer Series that brings creativity and liveliness to any life of prayer.

Mount Tabor Books Paraclete's newest series, Mount Tabor Books, focuses on the arts and literature as well as liturgical worship and spirituality, and was created in conjunction with the Mount Tabor Ecumenical Centre for Art and Spirituality in Barga, Italy.

Paraclete Recordings From Gregorian chant to contemporary American choral works, our recordings celebrate the best of sacred choral music composed through the centuries that create a space for heaven and earth to intersect. Paraclete Recordings is the record label representing the internationally acclaimed choir Gloriæ Dei Cantores, praised for their "rapt and fathomless spiritual intensity" by *American Record Guide*; the Gloriæ Dei Cantores Schola, specializing in the study and performance of Gregorian chant; and the other instrumental artists of the Gloriæ Dei Artes Foundation.

Paraclete Press is also privileged to be the exclusive North American distributor of the recordings of the Monastic Choir of St. Peter's Abbey in Solesmes, France, long considered to be a leading authority on Gregorian chant.

Paraclete Video Our DVDs offer spiritual help, healing, and biblical guidance for a broad range of life issues including grief and loss, marriage, forgiveness, facing death, bullying, addictions, Alzheimer's, and spiritual formation.

Learn more about us at our website:
www.paracletepress.com, or call us toll-free at 1-800-451-5006.

SCAN
TO
READ
MORE

YOU MAY ALSO BE INTERESTED IN . . .

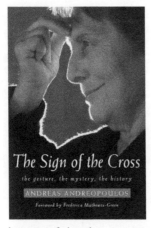

The Sign of the Cross
The Gesture, the Mystery, the History
Andreas Andreopoulos

ISBN: 978-1-55725-874-8 Paperback $17.99

The sign of the Cross is literally a tracing of the Cross of Christ onto the body. By so doing, Christians invite the mystery of the Cross into their everyday lives. Now and for the first time, young Greek scholar Andreas Andreopoulos explains the tremendous meaning, mystery, and history of this dramatic gesture shared by Christians worldwide. This readable account will fascinate and inspire all who desire to know more about the inherited spiritual practices of everyday life.

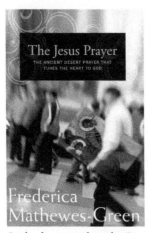

The Jesus Prayer
The Ancient Desert Prayer That Tunes the Heart to God
Frederica Mathewes-Green

ISBN: 978-1-55725-659-1 Paperback $16.99

Frederica Mathewes-Green offers the most comprehensive book to date on the Jesus Prayer—a spiritual jewel for anyone who yearns for a real and continuous presence with Christ. She illuminates the history, theology, and spirituality of Orthodoxy, so that the Prayer can be understood in its native context, and provides practical steps for making it a part of our being.

Available from most booksellers or through Paraclete Press:
www.paracletepress.com; 1-800-451-5006. Try your local bookstore first.

Lightning Source UK Ltd.
Milton Keynes UK
UKHW012022030821
388230UK00003B/889